A Series of Twelve Articles Introductory to the Study of the Bahá'í Teachings

Also from Westphalia Press
westphaliapress.org

A Series of Twelve Articles Introductory to the Study of the Bahá'í Teachings

---

by Charles Mason Remey

WESTPHALIA PRESS

An Imprint of Policy Studies Organization

A Series of Twelve Articles Introductory to the Study of the Bahá'í Teachings
All Rights Reserved © 2017 by Policy Studies Organization

Westphalia Press
An imprint of Policy Studies Organization
1527 New Hampshire Ave., NW
Washington, D.C. 20036
info@ipsonet.org

ISBN-13: 978-1-63391-565-7
ISBN-10: 1-63391-565-4

Cover design by Jeffrey Barnes:
jbarnesbook.design

Daniel Gutierrez-Sandoval, Executive Director
PSO and Westphalia Press

Updated material and comments on this edition
can be found at the Westphalia Press website:
www.westphaliapress.org

A SERIES OF TWELVE ARTICLES INTRODUCTORY
TO THE STUDY OF
THE BAHÁ'Í TEACHINGS

A SERIES OF TWELVE ARTICLES
INTRODUCTORY TO THE STUDY OF
THE BAHÁ'Í TEACHINGS

Treating briefly of the Revelation of Bahá'u'lláh,
History, Organization, Religious and Secular
Doctrines and Institutions.

by
CHARLES MASON REMEY

Approved by the
National Bahá'i Reviewing Committee of America
April, 1925

Printed by Tipografia Sordomuti, Firenze, Italia.

Series of twelve articles.

PREFACE.

This series of twelve articles, introductory to the Bahá'í Teachings, is compiled for the most part from writings circulated during the past decade or more, and is now published in order to meet the present increasing need for literature in the field of Bahá'í teaching. The material contained therein summarizes information which can be found in a less abridged form in the standard works of the Bahá'í Cause.

The writer wishes to express his deep appreciation of the assistance rendered him by Mrs H. Emogene Hoagg in the preparation of this book for press.

Florence, Italy,
May 15, 1925.   *C. M. R.*

The Reality of Religion.

'Abdú'l-Bahá

O army of life ! East and West have joined to worship stars of faded splendor and have turned in prayer unto darkened horizons. Both have utterly neglected the broad foundation of God's sacred laws, and have grown un-mindful of the merits and virtues of His religion. They have regarded certain customs and conventions as the immutable basis of the divine faith, and have firmly estab-lished themselves therein. They have imagined them-selves as having attained the glorious pinnacle of achieve-ment and prosperity when in reality they have touch-ed the innermost depths of heedlessness and deprived themselvels wholly of God's bountiful gifts.

The corner-stone of the religion of God is the acqui-sition of the divine perfections and the sharing in His manifold bestowals. The essential purpose of faith and belief is to ennoble the inner being of man with the outpourings of grace from on high. If this be not at-tained, it is indeed deprivation itself. It is the torment of infernal fire.

Wherefore it is incumbent upon all Bahá'ís to ponder this very delicate and vital matter in their hearts, that unlike other religions they may not content themselves with the noise, the clamor, the hollowness of religious doctrine. Nay, rather they should exemplify in every aspect of their lives those attributes and virtues that are born of God, and should arise to distinguish themselves by their goodly behaviour. They should justify their claim to be Bahá'ís by deeds and not by name. He is a true Bahá'í who strives by day and by night to progress and advance along the path of human endeavor, whose most cherished desire is so to live and act as to enrich and illuminate the world, whose source of inspiration is the essence of divine virtue, whose aim in life is so to conduct himself as to be the cause of infinite progress. Only when he attains unto such perfect gifts can it be said of him that he is a true Bahá'í. For in this holy dispensation, the crowning glory of bygone ages and cycles, true faith, is no mere acknowledgement of the unity of God, but rather the living of a life that will manifest all the perfections and virtues implied in such belief .... His holiness the Exalted One, may my life be a sacrifice unto him, and the Abhá Beauty, may my spirit be offered up in the path of his loved ones, have shown us the way of right behaviour, have guided us to the path of selfsacrifice, have taught us how to despise earthly rest and comfort, how to lay down our lives that others may prosper and succeed. That sanctified Being, despite the loftiness of His position, and the exaltation of his spirit, chose to be chained and fettered that we may obtain the light of divine guidance. All the days of his life he rested not for a moment, sought no repose, nor laid his head upon the couch of ease and security. His days were passed amidst afflictions and suffering : how can we prove ourselves worthy and yet remain inactive ? Surely it is but just that we arise to water this pure and widely-scattered seed, that we care for these saplings planted in the soil of hearts, that we dedicate ourselves wholly to the service of mankind. Then will the world be turned into a paradise, then will the surface of the earth mirror forth the glory of the Abhá Kingdom. Should this be otherwise, great will be our deprivation and grievous our loss.

O servant of Truth ! Wouldst thou obtain the sovereignty of earth and heaven, seek naught but true servitude at the threshold of the Abhá Beauty. Wouldst thou win the joy of liberty in this world and the next, desire not but submission unto his holy will. Wouldst thou discover the true way of God, follow the path of his Covenant. Wouldst thou behold the light of eternal splendor, fix thy gaze upon his bountiful grace vouchsafed from the Abhá Kingdom ».

INTRODUCTION

□□□□

THE MESSAGE

The Hope and Glad Tidings of this New Day

A general introduction

The Bahá'í Revelation

INTRODUCTION

THE MESSAGE.

At the present time the religious world is in a state of change. It is breaking away from the superstitions and the cold, hard and dead creeds and dogmas of the past, and it is awakening to and reaching out for a broader conception of truth, a dynamic religion which is at the same time liberal, tolerant and unsectarian. Nothing short of such a universal catholic faith can satisfy humanity in this day and age.

There are many philosophies. Because of man's finitude, infinite religion has taken upon itself many and varying forms of thought, but from the spiritual view-point of reality there is and can be but one religion, because there is but one God, and there is but one spiritual relation between *Him* and the individual souls of men. The knowledge of this spiritual relation between the Creator and the created, between the infinite divine being and man, is the one, the only and the true religion. It is the basic principle of the truth contained in all religious systems. Shorn of superstitions and imaginations and renewed by the divine spirit, it will be the religion of the future.

This present day is characterized by a great spirit-

ual awakening among the followers of all religions,
the like of which has never before been seen in the
world. This awakening is manifest among all people,
in all countries, and under all conditions. During the
past eighty years the world has entered upon a new
spiritual era. Many people who have made a study
of the domestic and foreign fields of religious work of
today realize this fact, notwithstanding their own
widely differing personal view-points. In the Christian
world we see the effect of this awakening in so con-
vincing a manner that illustrations are unnecessary.
In the other religions the same is clearly and strikingly
visible in the many changes and movements which, in
these latter years, have characterized Judaism, Islam-
ism, Hinduism, and latterly, the great progressive
awakening in China among the followers of Confucius.
This spiritual awakening is universal. It manifests itself
differently under varying conditions, — social, racial
and religious ; but considered as a whole, it indicates
that the soul of the world of humanity is now awake
searching truth and seeking freedom from the superstitions of the past, and that nothing short of the universal truth will appease its hunger and quench its
thirst.

There was a time when the various religions of the
world were considered as isolated and separate one
from another, with no connection between them ; but
now, in the light of this new day and age, all truth
is recognized to have emanated from the one source,
which is God. Many thinking people are now believ-
ing that religions in their purity are all based on the

same fundamental truths and are as parts of one great body organically connected. Each revelation of divine truth has been a step leading humanity to a higher conception of the Creator and his divine law, and preparing souls for the time when all men would be united in one great world universal faith, worshiping the one God in spirit and in truth. Great divine seers loom up in history as centers of religious inspiration. Then in the coming age another prophet appears, building upon the foundation of his predecessors, fulfilling their prophecies and accomplishing the hopes of their followers by leading humanity on a stage further in soul development. Each prophet prepared the way for the coming of the succeeding prophetic dispensation. In this way have all religious movements of the past been interrelated as integral parts of the foundation of God's universal kingdom here on earth, whose completed structure is destined to come as a great universal world religion, in which the prophecies and fruits of all religions will be realized.

The teachers and prophets, the founders of the world religions, have been seers as well as channels of truth to the people of their days. Through spiritual inspiration, understanding, and wisdom, they foresaw coming events and human conditions. They foretold this universal latter-day awakening of all people and demand for truth, and they foresaw the One who would meet and satisfy this demand for truth in the coming of another channel of divine grace, the great latter-day revelator. This holy personage, the latest of all Manifestations of the Word and power of God, they prophesied would arise with spiritual understanding and power, reveal and demonstrate the universal truth which exists in all religions, unite all men in faith, and establish the universal religion and the Kingdom of God on earth. That this Manifestation, the latest of all God's messengers, has come, and has founded his Cause in the world is the message that the Bahá'í Cause is giving to the world.

Each of the world's great divine teachers had a spiritual vision far in advance of the people of his time. These great God-men were independent of the human concepts and institutions of their days. They were creators of thought, morals, and social advancement. This progressive spirit of the divinely inspired founders of religions characterized each of the great religious movements during its earlier day. Later, as truth was supplanted by superstition in the minds of the people, the religions ceased to be independent institutions, — guiding the people — and became dependent institutions, dependent upon and catering to the thought and the imaginations of the people of the day. Its mission as a leader and creator of thought and morals was at an end, and instead of elevating the people it retarded their progress and became the cause of stagnation and disintegration. Such has been the development of superstitious theology in the many religions. Advancing civilization has had no more subtle or persistent enemy to contend with than the superstition of lifeless religious systems.

Foremost among the world problems of this day and age is the abolition of war and the establishment of international peace. In reviewing history one sees that national, racial and religious hatred and rancor have been one of the principal causes of war. Even at the present time the differing and opposing tenets, customs and morals held by the different religious teachings or philosophies are not only not working for peace upon earth, but through their separating influence upon men are actually holding people at variance, dividing humanity, and in many cases have been the direct cause of war in modern times. The object of the Bahá'í teaching is to strike a fatal blow at these prejudices. It not only seeks to eliminate the cause of strife, but in place of enmity it plants a virile and growing spirit of religious unity between the peoples reached.

The Bahá'í Revelation offers to the world a religious teaching applicable to the present modern needs of humanity. It is religion renewed. It teaches that all truth emanates from the one Word of God, through God's many mouth-pieces, His anointed ones, or prophets, and that truth has come into the world for the quickening of the soul of humanity, Thus the revealed teachings of all religions in their beginnings were pure, but as time passed man-created philosophy and thought crept in, killing the pure spirit of divine truth, until finally little remained save superstition, creed, dogma, and ceremony. Hence, a new spiritual quickening is necessary from age to age, and now again as in times past, God has revealed His Word anew for the whole world, that all men of all nations and races may receive more abundantly than ever before of His spirit. This He has accomplished through the three inspired revealers of the Bahá'í Cause : through the Báb, who was the herald and the " First Point „ of the revelation ; through Bahá'u'lláh, who was the great revealer of the Word ; through 'Abdú'l-Bahá, who was the expounder of the Word, and in whom all things were fulfilled. The Bahá'í organization has as its present head Shoghi Effendi, eldest grandson of 'Abdú'l-Bahá, appointed by 'Abdú'l-Bahá to be the first of a series of Guardians of the Cause—the function of this office and organization being to co-ordinate the spirit of the Bahá'í ideals and principles, and to promote the spirit of union and harmony between the peoples of different religions, races, nations and classes.

The Bahá'í principle of unity is not merely a negative suspension of inharmony or intolerance. It is a positive force for unity, potent and dynamic, which, as it grows, creates a new conciousness, transmuting destructive forces into constructive forces. It stands for progress, and is the promoter of all universal progressive thoughts of the age which are uniting the people of all races, religions and nations. This spiritual force is now needed by the world. Through it, the differences between eastern and western thought, manners and customs, and the lack of confidence between all people, are being changed and replaced by oneness of thought and action, and by confidence and fraternity. The Bahá'í Cause stands for :

1. The unity of all religions;
2. The political unity of all nations;

3. The social co-ordination and unity of groups com-
posing all peoples and races;
4. The unity of languages in one universal language;
5. Suffrage for women and men alike;
6. The advancement of all material institutions conducive to the general welfare of man, his enlightenment and progress;
7. World peace.

All of these much needed institutions are established
upon the divine foundation of spiritual or religious
unity between peoples, and in the fruition of the
Baháí service to humanity will appear the harvest of
the divine seeds sown in the hearts of the people by
the revealers of the Bahá'í Cause.

In this day the peoples of the world are being drawn
together by the material forces of civilization. Commercial and political relations have brought people of
all nations, races and religions together upon the plane
of their outer activities; but as yet they form a heter-
ogenous mixture, having no common or uniting consciousness or inner spiritual ground upon which to
build a fundamental unity. Such a divine spiritual
meeting-ground of common understanding or unity,
is now the most needed thing in the world. The time
is at hand for the people of the world to unite in all
matters, and first of all in religion since this is the most
potent factor in shaping the character of individuals
and groups. The good character of nations has been
built by religion, and it has been destroyed through
superstition, which is the lack of true religion.

The superstitious beliefs of the past have nothing to

offer to the world of today toward the solution of this mighty problem of a world unity. Each theological belief with its own particular theories, forms, and ceremonies was evolved under the limited human conditions of the past, before universal problems existed such as the world now faces. Therefore, the many theologies and various beliefs of the past have no relation to the present universal world-needs, nor power to influence mankind. The day of such religious superstitions is at an end, and this world is now ripe for the promulgating of a virile religious movement ; a religion ahead of the times, one whose teaching contains all the truths of the religions of the past, one which in independent of and not limited by past or present superstitions of man. Such a religion will lead the world onward, infusing into it the spiritual force necessary to reform its institutions, oriental and occidental, in their faith in God and confidence in one another, thus making a firm spiritual foundation for the coming great universal world-civilization.

The Bahá'í revelation is meeting this world-need and is ministering to it. It is not an eclectic philosophy gleaned from the past, neither is its sect. Rather it is a living spiritual force working in the heart of mankind. Because of its soul inspiring qualities and its spiritual power it appeals alike to the unschooled and the learned, to the masses and the few. The Báb, Bahá'u'lláh, and 'Abdú'l-Bahá, stand forth as divine teachers and leaders independent of the world's attitude and thought. They have created a living spiritual religious Cause that has spiritualized nature through the power of the Word of God. Like all divine teachers they were far ahead of their time. Peace, arbitration and an international language, in fact the vision of universal civilization were generally unthought of by the world when Bahá'u'lláh, over half a century ago, announced this spiritual message in which is incorporated the solution of the many questions which now occupy the minds of the greatest thinkers and philanthropists of the age. Upon every hand people are clamoring to understand more clearly the principles of peace and the oneness of humanity to which the Bahá'í leaders and their followers have borne witness by trials and suffering aud death.

Those who are familiar with the Bahá'í doctrines believe that through knowing, understanding, and living the principles of the Spiritual Kingdom, men will become united ; the various religious sects and cults will cease to exist as such, and all men will live as brothers. The Bahá'í Cause is actually bringing about this millennial condition. Through its teachings and influence the spiritual limitations of an undeveloped humanity are doomed to disappear, and truth, which is the love of God, will manifest itself here on this earth as brotherhood among men. The Bahá'í Cause is ministering to this great spiritual need of the day, by planting in the soul of the world a living invincible religion of brotherhood. Because of this reality and this human universal need, this Cause is destined to grow until it envelops the whole world, unites all men and leads them onward toward the age of spiritual enlightenment, prosperity and peace.

As the Bahá'í message is being given to people of each of the great world religions they are being called back to the original teachings of their holy books as given by their own prophets. They realize that the voice of the spirit of God spoke through them, and they understand all the prophets to be Manifestations of the one, only universal God, whose unsectarian truth is the foundation of all true religion.

. The Bahá'í Revelation teaches that, symbolically speaking, today is the time of judgment prophesied in the holy books of all peoples. The call of the Lord has again gone forth. People are hearing it, some are awakening to it and are arising to serve ; while other souls, as yet unreached by the verbal messages, are nevertheless unconciously responding to the spirit of this great Cause, and in their consciousness is being born the conviction and faith of the new day of God's bounty and peace upon earth.

That the Word of God has again been manifested to man, and that « The One » promised in the holy writings of all religions has come and has established the new and divine order of things, the Kingdom of God on earth, is the message which the Bahá'í Revelation is bringing to the world.

I.

THE BÁB

The Forerunner of Bahá'u'lláh and
The First Point of the Bahá'í Revelation
A Summary of his precursory Teachings and a brief outline of
the History of his Mission

THE BÁB.

The first divine teacher of the Bahá'í Revelation was M'irzá 'Alí Muhammad, known as the Báb. (¹) He was born in October, 1819, in the city of Shiráz, in southern Persia. His father, a Siyyid, or descendant of the prophet Muhammad, died during his infancy, and the young child was adopted into the family of a maternal uncle, a man of virtue, who reared him, giving him such elementary education in the Persian language as was customary among the sons of the merchant class to which he belonged. On attaining maturity, M'irzá 'Alí Muhammad went into business with his uncle and was for some time established in Bushire, upon the Persian Gulf. As a young man he was noted for purity, gentleness and charm. Even those who afterwards opposed and persecuted him and his followers most cruelly, never attacked his personal character. Much religious meditation, they claimed, had unbalanced his mind.

On May 23, 1844, moved by the Spirit of God, M'irzá 'Alí Muhammad declared his mission. At that time from various parts of Persia were gathered together in Shiraz eighteen spiritually prepared souls, men of religious wisdom to whom it had been given to understand divine realities. To these chosen disci-

(1) « Bab » is the Arabic and Persian word for door or gate.

ples M'irzá 'Alí Muhammad revealed his mission, as
the « door » (Báb) or forerunner of a great prophet
and teacher soon to appear. He, the Báb, had been
divinely sent as a herald to warn the people of the
coming of the great promised One, and to exhort
them to purify themselves and prepare for his advent.
One whom he entitled « He-whom-God-shall-manifest, » — the « Latter-Day Revelator, » « The Lord
of Hosts, » promised in the revealed writings of the
past — was soon to come and establish the new era
of the Kingdom of God upon earth.

These eighteen first disciples of the Báb were known
as the « Letters of the Living. » They, with himself
as « The Point, » formed the nucleus for the dissem-
ination of this new teaching. As soon as the Báb
had instructed these disciples in his simple doctrines,
he sent them into various parts of Persia with the
commission to teach and to proclaim his appearance.
He then, with one of his followers, went upon the
annual pilgrimage to Mecca, where, before a concourse
of pilgrims assembled from all parts of the Musl'im
world, he made his first public declaration. By the
time the Báb returned to Bushire in Persia, his Cause
was known in many parts of the country and was
gaining adherents so rapidly that the Musl'im clergy
were becoming alarmed lest through the rise of this
new cult they might lose their power and hold over
the people.

Shortly after landing in Bushire the Báb went to
Shiraz where his Cause was spreading. He was roughly
treated by the Musl'ims, placed under guard, and or-

dered to remain within the confines of his house. There, nevertheless, many had access to him, were attracted and believed in his teachings. Many of these were men of prominence and learning, while others were of the more humble walks of life. Through the power of divine love, the Báb overcame all obstacles ~~ ‥ ‥on the hearts of the people, quickening his followers with a spirit of most ardent devotion to his Cause.

Although the Báb was without learniug and school-ing, save that of a very elementary nature, he was so richly endowed with spiritual or inspirational wis-dom that he discomfited the learned Mullás until they feared discussion with him, lest the people should see the weakness of their argurments and the strength of his teaching. He wrote with the greatest rapidity and fluency, dictating both in public and private his many treatises upon intricate theological questions, taking the people away from speculative exegesis and instill-ing into their hearts spiritual wisdom, love and faith.

From Shiraz the Báb was, at the incitement of the opposing priesthood, taken in captivity from place to place, all of which strengthened and spread the Cause rather than impeded its growth. Thus seized and held as prisoner of State at the instigation of the Mullás, the Báb continued his mission of teaching the people. Even his captors could not resist the spirit which flowed from him, and many of them became his friends and staunch supporters, sacrificing all, even life, in his Cause.

The ministers of State being informed of the rapid growth of the Babí Movement, as it was called at that time, and fearing lest the Báb's presence in the cities of Persia would so agitate the clergy that they might possibly incite a religious uprising, an order was issued to the effect that the Báb should be imprisoned in the distant fortress of Makú in the mountain fastnesses of the extreme northwestern part of Persia. Thither he was taken a prisoner on this long cross-country journey. As the Báb passed through many cities, his fame continued to spread widely and many believed and followed his path.

Ere long the daily increase in the number of the Báb's followers in many parts of the land caused the Persian authorities to remove him from Makú to a still more remote imprisonment in the castle of Chi-rikh, in the foot hills of Mount Ararat, where he could be could be more closely guarded and less likely to communicate with the outside world. These precautions to curtail his influence were fruitless. His Cause grew, and his following having attained to great proportions the clergy became thoroughly alarmed and instigated a heresy trial and public examination of his doctrines. This investigation was held in the city of Tabri'z by the authority of the governor of that province, and before this tribunal the Báb was brought a prisoner.

All manner of insults and indignities were heaped upon him, and finally he was flogged, — one of the chief mullás applyng the rods with his own hands. After this the Báb was returned to his former prison in the castle of Chi-rikh.

About this time began the early general persecutions and massacres of the Babís in all Persia. Aroused by

their priests the fanatical Musl'ims fell upon the believers in many parts of the land, pillaging and burning their homes and torturing and murdering men,
women and children. These crimes are too revolting
to be mentioned in detail. Many are the accounts of
the marvelous courage and fortitude of even the children, not to mention that of the women and men.
These souls with the greatest calmness and joy sub-
mitted to the most fiendish tortures and death, rather
than recant or deny their faith, when denial would
have saved them. One's heart beats rapidly when he
realizes that through this suffering these martyrs were
lighting the way that the world might be prepared to
meet the One promised to appear who would establish
the new era of divine peace upon earth.

Sometimes Babí fugitives banded themselves together
to resist the attacks of the Musl'ims, and in some
instances they defended themselves valiantly and brave-
ly only to be slaughtered in the end by the over-
whelming number of their adversaries. That « the
blood of the martyrs is the seed of the church », is
again proven to the world in this day, for with the
shedding of each drop of Bábí blood the Cause gained
numbers of adherents. People who at first knew but
little of the Báb and his teachings, save that a prophet
had come, were confirmed in the faith and went forth
to serve, and die when called upon.

As one listens to the accounts of the lives of the
early Bábís, of their missions and labors, sufferings
and martyrdoms, he sees the wonderful spirit of the
love of God which actuated them as they responded to

the call. One is thrilled as he realizes that the day of a vital and burning faith, such as moved the apostles and fathers of old, has again appeared. From its inception, this latter-day religion has borne the same manner of spiritual fruit as the religions of the past bore in their earlier days.

Among the most prominent of the Báb's followers was Qurratu'l'Ayn, poet, orator and heroine of the Cause, who, after an eventful career in which she stood forth as a powerful exponent of the new faith, suffered a martyr's death. As a woman many decades ahead of her time, her life and example are an inspiration to people in all parts of the world, and especially to her sisters of the Orient, who, through the Cause for which she died are now being lifted from their former condition of ignorance and oppression into one of knowledge and freedom.

With the unfoldment of the Báb's message and the spiritual development of the followers, gradually he revealed his divine station more and more clearly to the people, until they saw him in his full capacity, not only as the forerunner of a great revelation to come, but himself as the « First Point » of this revelation. With this realization came greater and renewed confirmations and activities in teaching upon the part of the believers, causing renewals of hostilities upon the part of the Musl'im clergy.

Islám is the State religion of Persia, therefore that which shakes its power produces a like effect in the government. At length, seeing the Cause to be steadily on the increase, the priests brought such pressure to bear upon the government that the prime minister of the State ordered the Báb to be killed, hoping thus to put an end to the matter, and to place himself, the prime minister, and his political party, in security with the clergy and the people. Accordingly, the Báb was again removed from the prison of Chi-rikh and taken to Tabrí'z, the seat of the local government of the province. Here, on the 9th of July, 1850, he suffered martyrdom.

The Báb, with one of his most devoted followers, a youth of noble family, was conducted to an open square in the city and there the two were bound and suspended by ropes against a wall. A company of Armenian Christian soldiers was drawn up, and the order to fire given. When the smoke cleared, to the astonishment of all present, it was found that instead of harming the captives only the ropes had been severed and the two captives had dropped to the ground unhurt. So great was the consternation caused by this incident that the commander of the executing company refused to take further part in the affair, and another company of soldiers, native Musl'ims, was ordered out. The Báb and his disciple were again suspended before the wall, and the ensuing volleys riddled both bodies with bullets, causing instantaneous death. Later the remains were cast into a moat and there exposed to public view, as warning of the fate which awaited those who followed the new faith.

By night the body of the Báb was removed by some of the faithful, and swathed in silk was disguised as a bale of merchandise and deposited in a place of safety. As conditions and wisdom demanded, from time to time his hiding place was changed. Finally in the presence of a notable gathering of pilgrims from various parts of both the Orient and the Occident the body of the Báb was laid to rest by 'Abdú'l-Bahá in the « Shrine of the Báb » upon Mount Carmel in the Holy Land, now a Bahá'í place of worship, constantly visited by pilgrims from all parts of the world.

During the four years of the Báb's imprisonment, his numerous letters and epistles with the greatest difficulty were smuggled out of the prison and sent to the followers in various parts of the country. These writings contain his injunctions to the believers for their guidance and protection until the coming of « Him-whom-God-shall-manifest ».

One of the institutions of the Báb was the rearrangement of the calendar. This change was confirmed by Bahá'u'lláh, and the new calendar is beginning to be used by Bahá'ís. Eventually it will supersede the many systems now current. The Bahá'í era began with the year 1844 A.D., or 1260 of the Musl'im Hajira. The first day of the Bahá'í year falls on March 21, the day upon which the sun enters the sign of Aries and is commonly known as the first day of spring. The year is divided into nineteen months of nineteen days each, making in all 361 days to which are added four (every fourth year five) intercalary days to complete the 365 or 366 days of the year.

The Báb's ordinances were given for the people of his time, and were commensurable with the needs and conditions of the believers during the interim between his manifestation and the manifestation of the Greater One to come. The Báb was the « First Point » of this revelation, the precursor of the Greater One. In his teachings he reiterated again and again that, when « He-whom-God-shall-manifest » appeared, all should turn unto him, and that he would reveal teachings and ordinances which would replace the Bábí sacred literature.

Running through the Báb's writings are found countless allusions to the spiritual power, splendor and glory of Bahá'u'lláh, who was then in the world, but unknown to men. This holy personage was the inspiration of the Báb, to whom the Báb continually testified in the most eloquent and stirring of his verses, and of whom he bore witness by a life of suffering and imprisonment crowned by martyrdom.

PREFACE.

This series of twelve articles, introductory to the Bahá'í Teachings, is compiled for the most part from writings circulated during the past decade or more, and is now published in order to meet the present increasing need for literature in the field of Bahá'í teaching. The material contained therein summarizes information which can be found in a less abridged form in the standard works of the Bahá'í Cause.

The writer wishes to express his deep appreciation of the assistance rendered him by Mrs H. Emogene Hoagg in the preparation of this book for press.

Florence, Italy,
May 15, 1925.   *C. M. R.*

II.

BAHÁ'U'LLÁH.

« He Whom God Shall Manifest »
Whose coming was heralded by The Báb.
A brief Outline.
of the History of His Mission.

BAHÁ'U'LLÁH.

M'irzá Husayn 'Alí of Nur, more widely known as Bahá'u'lláh, was born in Tihrán, Persia, on the 12th of November, 1817. His family was one of wealth and note ; his father as well as other relatives having been ministers of the government, serving in various official capacities.

During Bahá'u'lláh's youth his father died leaving him, the eldest son, as the head of the family. Being of a contemplative disposition, the public life which his father had led had no allurements for Bahá'u'lláh. He chose, instead a life of comparative retirement, managing the family estates and affairs and supervising the education of his brothers and sisters. It is recorded that even in very early youth the marks of wisdom and distinction were upon him.

In his home Bahá'u'lláh was taught the Persian language, but he never attended any school or college. Through inspiration the deepest of spiritual mysteries were his. Later these basic principles of being are revealed with power and force in his writings. These truths are the foundation of the Bahá'í Cause. They are the living, spiritual principles of existence. Their understanding appeals to and satisfies the soul and meets the moral and spiritual needs of life. His knowledge came from the source of all knowledge and is the source of knowledge for all.

At the time the Báb made his declaration and sent

his disciples forth from Shi'ráz, Bahá'u'lláh, then about twenty-seven years of age, was residing in Tihrán. When the glad tidings of the Báb's manifestation reached the capitol, Bahá'u'áh was among the first to respond to the call, and in turn he proclaimed the Cause and upheld it publicly. He visited the city of Núr, the home of his family, and other neighboring cities and towns where he engaged in expounding the Báb's teachings, later returning to Tihrán, there again to take up the work of teaching the Cause.

The Báb and Bahá'u'lláh had no family connection whatever, the former being of Arabic-Persian descent, while the latter was of ancient Persian lineage. These two personages never met in person, yet in spirit they were intimate, contacting even in their deepest thoughts and inspirations.

Shortly after the Báb's martyrdom came the greatest persecution of the followers. Even to be suspected of being a believer was, in many cases, sufficient to cause the extinction of an entire family. In Tihrán some eighty believers were handed over by the government officials to the Musl'ims, each being subjected to some unique torture before the final slaying. Each calamity was followed by one more terrible, yet through all the wonderful hope of the Promised One to come and the enthusiastic love and devotion of the followers to the memory of their martyred master upheld and strengthened them to meet every form of persecution.

In the midst of these troubles Bahá'u'lláh w asarrested, prison placed in chains and cast into underground prison for four months in Tihrán. Later on he was sent

by the royal order into exile to Baghdád, in Asiatic
Turkey. There it was thought he would be so far
removed from the Bábís in Persia as to destroy his
prestige as leader among them.

After the fury of the massacres of 1851-1852 the
Babís were in a deplorable condition. Many of the
disciples and personal associates of the Báb had been
martyred, while on account of the troubles the few
remaining ones who had personally been taught by
him were more or less cut off from association with
the younger followers. It had not been possible to
disseminate beyond a very limited circle the writings of
the Báb, so that the vast majority of the believers
knew little of the depth of his real teaching. In
addition, they were actuated by a powerful spirit of
devotion to their Cause; a devotion which, because of
its very intensity, led them into difficulties.

This was the condition that prevailed when Bahá'u'-
lláh reached Baghdád. Immediately he directed his
attention and energy toward bringing knowledge and
assurance to the followers. He taught them the real
or spiritual significance of the Báb's teachings, and
little by little, through understanding, the hitherto
undirected enthusiasm of the followers found power
in restraint and in united and directed efforts at promulgating the Cause.

As the believers increased in number the anger of
the Musl'im clergy was aroused and stirred, and
this in turn gave rise to other serious difficulties.
Then Bahá'u'lláh was led to seek a solitary retreat in
the mountain fastness of Kurdistán where he remained

for two years in spiritual preparation for his coming
manifestation and ministry. Upon his return to Baghdád, great was the joy of the Bábis. By that time
they were realizing their spiritual strength and they
welcomed their teacher and chief with all the fervor
and enthusiasm of oriental devotees.

These developmens were closely watched by the
Musl'im priests. Fearful of the loss of their own
hold upon the people, which they saw waning as the
light of this new teaching spread, these priests now
incited the government against Bahá'u'lláh, with the
result that an international arrangement was formu-
lated by which he was ordered to proceed to Constantinople, there to await the pleasure of the Ottoman
Sultan, to who he became temporally subject.

Upon hearing that Bahá'u'lláh was to be removed
from Baghdád, the believers were plunged into grief,
and a number of them prepared to accompany him.
When, in obedience to the summons of the Sultán,
Bahá'u'lláh left Baghdád, previous to starting on his
long journey he encamped a short distance from the
city in a garden called El Ridván. There, to the most
trusted of these followers, Bahá'u'lláh revealed himself
and his mission; that he was the Promised One foretold by the Báb; that he was the One promised by
all the propnets to appear in the latter days and establish God's kingdom, the great universal brotherhood
of nations; that he was the One through whose inspired guidance the difficulties of the believers would
be removed; and that by steadfastly and unitedly
following whose injunctions those blessings for which

the believers had hoped, suffered and prayed would be realized. This hope he extended to the adherentes exhorting them to renew their energies, faith and assurance. The coming of Bahá'u'lláh was the goal toward which the Babís had directed their attention. Now, having attained to the meeting of the Promised One, the believers found themselves upon the threshold of an outlook so vast, and of a work so great, that it was only by the sustaining power of Bahá'u'lláh and by dependence upon him that they were able to face and surmount the difficulties wich confronted them.

Traveling overland and by sea, Bahá'u'lláh and his band of followers, after a fatiguing journey reached Constantinople. Here the exiles remained for several months under military surveillance before they were sent under military escort to Adrianople, in the interior of Roumelia. Bahá'u'lláh remained in Adrianople for five years, during which time the Cause grew in numbers and in strength. Through personal contact, those who were with him waxed strong in the light of his wisdom, while those at a distance had their souls made strong and steadfast through his written teachings; for in him all found the realization of the spiritual power, glory, and majesty of « Him-whom-God-shall-manifest. »

Bahá'u'lláh achieved his work only under the greatest difficulties. He was opposed on all sides. Finally, the spread of the faith created trouble with the Turkish government, and an order was issued to send Bahá'u'lláh as a prisoner to the fortress of Akka on

the coast of Syria. It was in the summer of 1863
that Bahá'u'lláh and about seventy of his followers-
men, women, and children, landed in Akka. Akka is
the Acre of the time of the crusaders, more anciently
known as Ptolemais. For a number of years prior to
Bahá'u'lláh's arrival, the fortress off Akka had been
used as a prison and a place of exile to ·which the
Sultán of Turkey sent his political opponents. Here
Bahá'u'lláh and his people wers thrust into two rooms
of the barrack prison. In this strict confinement, with
poor and insufficient food, and water not fit to drink
fever and sickness broke out among the believers.
Their sufferings were most intense, yet through all
they were spiritually in the greatest joy and peace,
for they realized that only by meeting the very worst
of this world's conditions could Bahá'u'lláh change
those conditions; while as for themselves, they were
only too happy and contented to share his sufferings.

After two years of rigid confinement in prison Bahá'-
u'lláh was allowed to live in a house provided for him
and his family. There he was in close confinement
for seven years. His follwers entered into various
occupations in the town and vicinity, and the ·mate-
rial condition of the community was greatly improved.
Then came pilgrims from various countries to him,
and quickened by his power they went forth to proclaim his Cause in the uttermost parts of the earth.
Besides those who saw him personally, Bahá'u'lláh
reached thousands in distant lands and satisfied their
thirst for knowledge through his tablets, which were

epistles of exhortation, advice, and explanation written in response to letters from believers and seekers.

During the latter years of his ministry, Bahá'u'lláh was allowed to spend much time in the country in the vicinity of Akka, even visiting Haifa and Mt. Carmel. At the villa of Bahjí, situated on the plain of Akka, he departed this life in the month of May, 1892. He suffered forty years of hardship, imprisonment and exile that the soul of the world might be quickened and that spiritual unity and peace might prevail on earth. The shrine of Bahá'u'lláh at Bahjí is now a place of worhip and prayer, and greatly venerated by the many pilgrims who yearly visit it from all parts of the world.

Every religion has had its birth in the advent of its divine founder. Through the labors of its early adherents it grew and developed, bringing forth its fruits in the institutions and civilization which grew up and formed about it. This was its golden age. Then followed a period in which the faith of the people grew cold, spirituality waned, morals suffered, and religion, losing its spirit, became a form. Then the souls of the people became starved and their condition needed the ministration of another prophet who, in due time, appeared and lifted them a step higher toward the coming of The Kingdom upon earth.

Each prophet has been a link in the great chain of revelators, completing the work and fulfilling the words of his predecessor and preparing the way for others to come after him. Thus have all the prophet Manifestations of the past prepared the way for the coming

of the great teacher of this day and age, Bahá'u'lláh,
whose mission is to unite those now following the
many religions into one brotherhood and one universal
faith. Through Bahá'u'lláh this great latter-day teaching was given to man. His function was that of
the revealer. As a man he lived a life in harmony
with his conception of the requirements of his oriental
environment, yet as the revelator, the mouthpiece of
the spirit, his teachings are universally applicable to
all peoples under all conditions. With the close of
his ministry this latter-day revelation was complete.
The next step in development of the Cause was that
of explaining, establishing, and demonstrating these
revealed truths in the world of practice. For the ac-
complishment of this, 'Abdú'l-Bahá, the son of Bahá-
'u'lláh, was the chosen instrument.

As one studies 'Abdú'l-Bahá's teachings and his life
of service to humanity, one becomes conscious of the
spirit of Bahá'u'lláh which was manifested in him. In
'Abdú'l-Bahá's presence one became conscious of the
deepest feeling of respect, veneration, and even awe, yet
not the awe which held one at a distance — for within
'Abdú'l-Bahá's soul there burned such a fire of divine
love that very few escaped its power of attraction. The
awakened sould realized that 'Abdú'l-Bahá understood
the spiritual condition of man and that he was the
divine physician who, through the love of God, was
healing the soul of man of the. disease of spiritual
ignorance and superstition and inharmony. He ministered to each in accordance with the needs of the in-
divual. Often at the time one did not understand why

'Abdú'l-Bahá advised as he did, but later all became clear when, by carrying out his instructions, one realized the depth of his understanding and the profoundness of his wisdom. 'Abdú'l-Bahá's vision penetrated the soul and understood its condition. His balm was summed up in the word love. Divine love annihilates worry and kills fear, and when it takes possession of the soul it brings with it the peace of God.

Through the Báb the way was made ready and prepared for the coming of Bahá'ulláh. Through Bahá-'u'lláh divine knowledg was revealed to man ande the spiritual law of the Kingdom given to the world for this day and age. Through 'Abdú'l-Bahá's life of service to God and man the way was made plain for all, and the Cause of God was established upon earth.

III.

'ABDÚ'L-BAHÁ.

The Center of The Covenant of Bahá'u'lláh,
The Interpreter of The Revealed Word,
The One, who was appointed to
establish The Bahá'í Cause in the world.

A brief outline of His Mission

'ABDÚ'L-BAHÁ

'Abdú'l-Bahá, also known as 'Abbás Effendi, the eldest son of Bahá'u'lláh, was born in Tihrán, Persia, on the 23rd day of May, 1844, the very day upon which the Báb made his declaration to his disciples in Shi'rás.

At a very early age 'Abdú'l-Bahá was called upon to share the sufferings of his father. When Bahá'-u'lláh's persecution began with his imprisonment in Tihrán, and exile to Baghdád, his family property was confiscated, even to personal effects and belongings, and the members of his family suffered intensely for the bare necessities ot life. 'Abdú'-Bahá's schooling was interrupted in his childhood by these persecutions, and afterward he never attended a school. However, through his constant communion with Bahá'u'lláh, through whom his inspiration came, an understanding, wisdom, and knowledge of all things were his.

'Abdú'l-Bahá accompanied Bahá'-u'lláh upon his winter journey from Tihrán to Baghdád, and during the years of exile there and later in Adrianople and in Akka, was constantly at Bahá'u'lláh's right hand, serving and helping him in his work of teaching the people.

'Abdú'l-Bahá was the first to recognize the divine station of Bahá'u'lláh. He was the first soul quickened by the life-giving spirit of Bahá'u'lláh, and he was the first to arise in the service of the Kingdom. In 'Abdú'l-Bahá's life of devotion to the Cause and his practice of the precepts of Bahá'u'lláh, the perfect life of the eternal Kingdom was manifest, and in him all things were realized and accomplished.

'Abdú'l-Bahá took upon himself the task of relieving Bahá'u'lláh of all possible cares of daily life, so that Bahá'u'lláh might devote himself entirely to his mission. During the imprisonment in Akka, when hardship and sickness were encompassing the believers on every side, it was 'Abdú'l-Bahá who, through his buoyancy of spirit, gave courage to the distressed ones. He nursed the sick, and through the touch of his hand imparted strength to the weak ; while the light of his great love illumined all and impowered them to overcome their ills.

In the written testament of Bahá'u'lláh, as well as in his spoken teachings which have been handed down to us through those who were near him, he appointed his son 'Abdú'l-Bahá to succeed him in his spiritual mission, and designated him as the one who should continue and complete his work in the world. The father's mantle fell upon the shoulders of the son. The staff of Bahá'u'lláh passed into the hands of 'Abdú'l-Bahá, and the spirit of God which spoke through Bahá'u'lláh, revealing truth to the world, later was manifested to humanity through 'Abdú'l-Bahá's life of service to the Cause.

With the passing of Bahá'u'lláh (May, 1892), began 'Abdú'l-Bahá's divine mission as « The Center of the

Covenant. » When he arose, invested with the power of the Spirit, then began the third period of the establishment of the Kingdom here among men. 'Abdú'l-Bahá stood as the exponent of a spiritual principle, a great divine power. The Bahá'ís had the uttermost esteem, love and veneration for 'Abdú'l-Bahá. To them he was the living testimony of Bahá'u'lláh, their divine friend, counselor, and spiritual guide.

In looking toward 'Abdú'l-Bahá as the expounder of divine wisdom, his followers revered and glorified the divine light of Bahá'u'lláh which manifested through him. No soul could fathom the depths into which 'Abdú'l-Bahá saw, nor the profoundness of his realization of the suffering condition of mankind. He felt the hunger and thirst of soul of humanity for spiritual rest, and upon his brow was written her silent agony. When 'Abdú'l-Bahá spoke, his listeners realized that he was fairly charged with the positive life-force of the Kingdom. In every glance and movement he manifested the joy of the Lord, and as he showed forth this love and joy in his many deeds of kindness, his spirit penetrated the hearts of those who came in contact with him, and they in turn went forth filled with his spirit to work and to serve in his path.

The pilgrim discovered that 'Abdú'l-Bahá impressed his hearers by calling forth a response from within the soul of each individual seeker, not by projecting his own ideas or personality upon them. The direct influence of the will of one personality upon another is transitory and without lasting benefit. But how

different was the message of the spirit speaking through
the life and words of 'Abdú'l-Bahá! He had a
message for every one, and as the soul of the seeker
met in spirit the soul of 'Abdú'l-Bahá, he felt a new
force added to his nature, and he went forth quickened, alive and aflame with the love of God, desirous
of serving God by calling humanity to His Kingdom.

'Abdú'l-Bahá came with the power of God to live
and manifest the life of the Kingdom. This he demonstrated to the world, for through his ministry all
things were accomplished as intended and revealed by
Bahá'u'lláh. Bahá'u'lláh alluded to 'Abdú'l-Bahá in
the most exalted terms in both his spoken and written
word, distinctly stating that he, 'Abdú'l-Bahá was not
one of the creatures, but unique aud different from
all mankind in his divine station. 'Abdú'l-Bahá pre-
ferred to allude to himself as « 'Abdú'l-Bahá », which
translated means « The servant of Bahá (God). « Thus
the name 'Abdú'l-Bahá, by which he was so widely
known, was of his own choosing, not one given him
by Bahá'u'-lláh.

Almost the entire life of 'Abdú'l-Bahá was passed
undes the temporal law as a religious prisoner. At
times he was only under military surveillance, and
again imprisoned behind barred doors. Yet despite
these physical hindrances his spiritual work prospered
and his message of glad-tidings went the world around,
taking with it the peace of the spirit to thousands of
souls of every race and religion. At times, on account
of the troubles brought on by the opposing people, it
was impossible for the believers to visit 'Abdú'l-Bahá.

At one time some of his followers were cast into prisson, and at another time some of the believers were forced to flee from the Holy Land and seek refuge in Egypt. Nevertheless, through all trials and troubles, 'Abdúl'-Bahá went steadily forward accomplishing his work, the number of his opposers decreasing and the number of his sympathizers increasing, until he clearly showed to all that his Cause was not dependent upon earthly prosperity for its growth, nor did opposition hinder its spread.

'Abdú'l-Bahá changed the world by infusing spiritual wisdom into men's souls. He taught the people through leading them, rather than by trying to force them ; through winning souls by the spirit, rather than by argument.

Many beautiful and touching incidents are related by the people of Akka of the way in which, through long-suffering and kindness, 'Abdú'l-Bahá won the hearts of those who, because of their prejudice, formerly were his enemies. Caring for the sick and protecting ·the oppressed formed a large· part of his daily duties. One of the titles applied to him by the indigent Arabs was, « Faher of the Poor ». His personal needs and those of his family were few. In reality, that which he possessed was for the benefit of all, while he was but the guardian of it. No ono knew how many children he was educating ; how many needy and infirm ones he healed and fed. 'Abdú'l-Bahá demonstrated to the world that there in neither virtue nor disgrace in either riches or poverty ; and that man, either in need or in plenty, should utilize his little or his much in glorifyng God through serving humanity.

'Abdú'l-Bahá had many expenses in connection with the carrying on of the work of the Cause. The American Bahá'ís testify that he very rarely permitted any of them to share in carrying the burden of the work in the East, though in rare instances he did accept contributions for various purposes.

'Abdú'l-Bahá was married. He had four daughters, three of whom have families. Through his home life 'Abdú'l-Bahá as a devoted husband and a loving father, taught a lesson to the people of both the East and the West. He taught monogamy, and that woman should be man's intellectual, moral and spiritual companion as well as the mother of his children. He taught in these days of marital unrest that marriage, to bear the fruits of happiness and contentment, should be founded upon a spiritual basis and not alone upon a physical one.

'Abdú'l-Bahá was an exile from his country for seventy years, and was held in the fortress of Akka as a religious prisoner from 1868 until the summer of 1908, when the Turkish Constitution was established. With this political change of affairs in Turkey he was freed from confinement and from military surveillance.

'Abdú'l-Bahá expressed perfect manhood. The vigor of a fully developed physical, intellectual and spiritual power was apparent in his every movement; yet with this was a delicacy, a sensibility and an intuition which manifested the inspiration that dominated him. In him was all the dignity and majesty of a king combined with the humbleness of the servant; and upon his brow was the strength and force of the ancient Mosaic patriarchal type of man, counterbalanced by the gentleness of a child.

In contacting in spirit with the soul of 'Abdú'l-Bahá, and in realizing his great love for humanity, it was as though another and new dimension were added to the soul of the visitant seeker for truth, and old conditions of doubt and uncertainty were replaced by poise and assurance. 'Abdú'l-Bahá's mission was to teach man to bring the love of the Kingdom into every day life and to manifest it in every thought, word and deed.

It is in the little things and the numerous details of life that the test comes in applying spiritual teachings. In the life of 'Abdú'l-Bahá it was through the seemingly small things that his great spirit manifested itself and went out with a penetrating power to the souls of those who allowed themselves to come within the radius of its activity. In his presence it was as if a refreshing breeze, a spiritual force, proceeded from his heart to that of the seeker, — a mysterious force carrying strength to the weak and guidance to the strong.

'Abdú'l-Bahá's every word, look and gesture manifested his spirit, and while this spirit was the most elusive and difficult of all things but when once one recognized it, it was the most tangible of realities, for it was the very essence of the light of the soul of humanity proceeding from him who was the center of divine life and guidance.

After his release from confinement in the fortress
of Akka, 'Abdú'l-Bahá made few changes in his daily
life, but many more of his followers could visit him
than formerly, consequently his duties and labors
increased. He gave up his residence in Akka, and
after living for some months in the neighboring town
of Haifa, went to Egypt, and later on to Europe and
America, ever engaged in the labors of his spiritual
mission. During the eight months which he spent in
America in 1912 he traveled from coast to coast, visiting most of the principal cities, and delivered addresses wherever the doors were thrown open to him.
These addresses were given in churches of many de-
nominations, in synagogues, universities and before
various organizations. Wherever he went he brought
the quiet joy and assurance of God's Kingdom to the
hearts of the people.

After leaving America 'Abdú'l-Bahá made a tour of
Europe and spent some time in Egypt, everywhere
demonstrating and giving forth the spirit of the Bahá'í
Cause.

The few months prior to the war found 'Abdú'l-
Bahá back again in the Holy Land on Mt. Carmel,
where, cut off from the outside world, he remained
during the years of the great combat, ministering to
and feeding the starving people, numbers of whom
would otherwise have died of hunger and want. Then
the post-war conditions in Palestine made it possible
again for 'Abdú'l-Bahá's friends to visit him and receive his teachings.

When the British army entered Palestine, the conquerors came in contact with the Master, 'Abdú'l-Bahá, and in recognition of his service for the betterment of humananity, the knighthood of the British Empire was conferred upon him, and this he graciously accepted.

As the time for his departure from this world drew nigh, 'Abdú'l-Bahá made ready all of his affairs, and then quickly, and without any apparent bodily illness, in the very early hours of the morning of November 28th, 1921, his spirit took its flight from this mortal realm. On the following morning his remains were laid in a tomb adjacent to that of the Báb, in the Bahá'í Shrine upon Mt. Carmel, - the officials of Palestine, British and native, attending, while the funeral services were conducted by the united cooperation of the clergy of the Musl'im, Christian and Jewish religions.

'Abdú'l-Bahá's tomb, like that of the Báb and Bahá'u'lláh, is visited daily by the friends of the Cause, and is a sanctuary from which continually arises the prayers and supplications of the faithful for the people of the world and for the triumph of God's kingdom on earth.

The shock and deep grief of the Bahá'ís in all parts of the world caused by 'Abdú'l-Bahá's departure, was somewhat assuaged by the provisions which he had made in his will and testament for the guardianship and the continued guidance and development of the Cause. As the Báb covenanted regarding Bahá'u'llah, and Bahá'u'lláh appointed 'Abdú'l-Bahá « The Center of his Covenant », so 'Abdú'l-Bahá left full and complete instructions for the organization of the Cause under an appointed « Guardian », the primal branch branched forth from the tree of the new covenant of of Abhá. Now the Cause is functioning about this organic center of guidance, which is the heart of the body-Bahá'í in the world, — a living spiritual organism destined to grow and expand until it fills the entire world, bringing the peace and joy of the Lord to peoples of all races, nation and religions.

IV.

GUARDIANSHIP AND ORGANIZATION.

Shoghi Effendi the First Guardian.
The Protection. Systematizing,
administration and growth of
The Bahá'í Cause.

THE GUARDIANSHIP AND ORGANIZATION OF THE BAHÁ'Í CAUSE.

'Abdú'l-Bahá covenanted in his Will that after his passing there would be a continued and a perpetuated center of guidance for the Cause, a Guardian, the office to be hereditary. The Guardian is to be the center about whom the Bahá'ís should revolve, the one whose mission would be to direct, continue and further the work of the Cause ; the one upon whom the mantle of the spirit would descend to protect, guide and inspire the people of the Cause and lead them onward in their spiritual work.

'Abdú'l-Bahá appointed his eldest grandson Shoghi Effendi to be the first of this line of Guardians. Shoghi Effendi descends on his mother's side from Bahá'u'lláh through 'Abdú'l-Bahá, and upon his father's side from a collateral branch of the family of the Báb. *

Upon him devolves the duty of establishing the organization of the Cause as outlined in the will of Abdú'l-Bahá.

The appointment of the Guardian was made by 'Abdú'l-Bahá in his Will in the following words:

O my loving friends! After the passing away of this wronged one, it is incumbent upon the Branches and

---

* The Báb's only child, a son, died in infancy.

Twigs of the sacred Lote-Tree (i. e. the relatives of the Báb and Bahá'u'lláh), the Hands of the Cause of God and the loved ones of the Abhá Beauty, to turn to Shoghi Effendi — the youthful Branch, branched from two hallowed and sacred Lote-Trees (the Báb and Bahá'u'lláh) and the fruit grown from the union of the two offshoots of the Tree of Holiness, as he is the sign of God, the chosen Branch, the Guardian of the Cause of God, he unto whom all the Branches, the Twigs, the Hands of the Cause of God and his loved ones must turn. He is the expounder of the words of God, and after him will succeed the first born of his lineal descendants....

The sacred and youthful Branch, the Guardian of the Cause of God, as well as the Universal Assembly (Baytu'l-'Adl) to be universally elected and established, are both under the care and protection of the Abhá Beauty, under the shelter and unerring guidance of His Holiness the Exalted One. May my life be offered up for them both! Whatsoever they decide is of God.

O ye beloved of the Lord! It is incumbent upon the Guardian of the Cause of God to appoint in his own lifetime him that shall become his successor, that differences may not arise after his passing. He that is appointed must manifest in himself detachment from all worldly things, must be the essence of purity, must show in himself the fear of God, knowledge, wisdom and learning. Thus, should the first born of the Guardian of the Cause of God not manifest in himself the truth of the words, « the child is the secret essence of its sire », that is, should he not inherit of the spiritual within him (the Guardian), and his glorious lineage not be matched with a goodly character, then must the Guardian of the Cause choose another Branch to succeed him.

« *The Hands of the Cause of God must elect from their own number nine persons that shall at all times be occupied in the important service of the work of the Guardian of the Cause of God. The election of these nine must be carried, either unanimously or by majority from the company of the Hands of the Cause of God, and these, whether unanimously or by majority vote, must give their assent to the choice of the one whom the Guardian of the Cause of God hath chosen as his successor. This assent must be given in such wise that the assenting and dissenting voices may not be distinguised (i. e. by secret ballot)* ».

Important among the Bahá'í institutions mentioned in the writings of Bahá'u'lláh is that of the Baytu-'l-'Adl (Spiritual Assembly), the duty of which would be the service and the direction of the Cause and its furtherance. The plan for the development and founding of this Assembly was left to 'Abdú'l-Bahá, and in his Will and Testament is further unfolded the plan for this spiritual institution. The organization calls for two distinct bodies functioning with the Guardian, upholding the divine ideals of the religion ; (1) The « Hands of the Cause of God » ; and (2) The Spiritual Assemblies.

1. The « Hands of the Cause of God » is to be a body of tried teachers and servants of the Cause, severed from the world, elevated to this station by appointment by the Guardian, and chosen by him because of spiritual policies and noble characteristics.

Of the Hands of the Cause of God 'Abdú'l-Bahá writes in his Will as follows:

O friends! The Hands of the Cause of God must be nominated and appointed by the Guardian of the Cause of God. The obligation of the Hands of the Cause of God is to diffuse the divine fragrances, to edify the souls of men and to be, at all times and under all circumstances, sanctified and detached from earthly things. They must manifest the fear of God by their conduct, their manners, their deeds and their words.

This body of the Hands of the Cause of God is under the direction of the Guardian of the Cause of God. He must continually urge them to strive and endeavor to the utmost of their ability to diffuse the sweet savors of God, and to guide all the people of the world, for it is the light of divine guidance that causes all the universe to be illumined.

2. A series of spiritual assemblies, local and national, with one international assembly hare to be established. The local spiritual assemblies in each Bahá'í community, elected by the people, have charge of local Bahá'í activities. The National Spiritual Assembly, elected by representatives of the people in each country, is above the local assemblies and has charge of the general affairs which pertain to the Bahá'í activities in that land. The Universal or International Spiritual Assembly, the members of which are selected by the national bodies, is above the national spiritual assemblies. Already Shoghi Effendi has inaugurated a system of local and national assemblies, and the friends of the Cause are now looking toward his future work in the further

development of these spiritual institutions which are at the head of the organization of the Cause. Of the organization of these spiritual assemblies 'Abdú'-Bahá wrote in his testament as follows:

And now, concerning the Assembly (Baytu'l-'Adl) which God hath ordined as the source of all good and freed from all error, it must be elected by universal suffrage, that is by the believers. Its nembers must be manifestations of the fear of God, and the day-springs of knowledge and understanding, must be steadfast in God's faith, and the well wishers of all mankind. By this Assembly is meant the Universal Assembly: that is, in each country a secondary Assembly must be instituted, and these secondary assemblies must elect the members of the Universal one.

Unto this body all things must be referred. Il enacteth all ordinances and regulations that are not to be found in the explicit holy texts. By this body all difficult problems are to be resolved, and the Guardian of the Cause is the sacred head and distinguished member for life, of that body. Should he not attend in person its deliberations, he must appoint one to represent him.... This Assembly enacteth the laws and the executive enforceth them. The legislative body must reinforce the executive, the executive must aid and assist the legislative body so that, through the close union and harmony of these two forces, the foundation of firmness and justice may become firm and strong, that all the regions of the world may become even as paradise itself.

Unto the Most Holy Book every one must turn, and all that is not expressly recorded therein must be refer-

red to the Universal Assembly. That which this body, either unanimouly or by majority, doth carry, that is verily the truth and the porpose of God himself. Whoso doth deviate therefrom is verily of them that love discord, hath shown forth malice, and turned away from the Lord of the Covenant.

It is incumbent upon the members (of the Universal Assembly) to gather in a certain place and deliberate upon all problems which have caused difference, questions that are obscure, and matters that are not expressly recorded in The Book. Whatsoever they decide has the same effect as the text itself. And inasmuch as this Assembly hath pover to enact laws that are not expressly recorded in the Book, and bear upon daily transactions, so also it has power to repeal the same. Thus for example, the Assembly enacteth today a certain law and a hundred years hence, circumstances having changed and the conditions being altered, another Assembly will then have power, according to the exigencies of the time, to alter that law. This it can do, because that law formeth no part of the divine explicit text. The Assembly is both the initiator and the abrogator of its own laws.

Shoghi Effendi at the time of the passing of 'Abdú-'l-Bahá was but twenty-five years of age. He has the love, devotion and confidence of the Bahá'ís in all countries. In his decisions they see great Bahá'í wisdom. They are doing all in their power to support and aid him in his great work, strong in the assurance that this is the Cause of God and that its growth and spiritual victory over the irreligion of the world, with its superstition and misery, is assured and confirmed and cannot fail.

One of the questions the Bahá'is are often asked is regarding the number of those who profess this faith. The strength of this Cause is a spiritual one, not to be measured numerically. Even were it possible to know the exact number of Bahá'ís in the world, this record would be valid but a short while, because the Cause is growing continually, interest in it is increasing and the hearts of people are daily becoming more attracted and more confirmed in the truth.

The Bahá'ís are widely distributed throughout the world. During the days of the Báb, his Cause was confined principally to Persia, although he had adherents also in neighboring countries. With the rise of Bahá'u'lláh this field of work was extended, the Bahá'í teachers went north in Caucasia, Russia and Turkestan, south into India, east into Burma, and later on into China. With Bahá'u'lláh's exile in Turkey, Roumelia and Syria, his Cause spread in those countries as well as in Egypt and in Arabia.

The establishment of the Bahá'í Cause in the West has been accomplished under the ministry of 'Abdú'l-Bahá. In the year 1894, a small group of people in the city of Chicago became interested in the revelation. Later, similar groups were formed in New York, Washington and San Francisco. In the winter of 1898-99, the first band of American Bahá'í pilgrims crossed the seas to visit 'Abdú'l-Bahá, then in exile in the Holy Land. Up to that time the communication between the American Bahá'ís and 'Abdú'-Bahá had been by writing only. Then, with the added impetus given by contact with 'Abdú'l-Bahá these American pilgrims returned to the West with renewed zeal and desire to spread the Cause.

From the enthusiasm of this first band of travelers, new centers for teaching were founded in France, England and America. From this nucleus have developed believers in all parts of the United States, in Canada, Mexico, Hawaii, Japan and Australia, New Zealand and South America and the West Indies, as well as in various parts of Germany, Switzerland and Italy. During this period of growth, several Bahá'í teachers from the Orient have traveled through Europe and America, instructing and teaching the people, and helping to establish new centers. Likewise, teachers from the Occident have journeyed and taught in the oriental countries. Quietly and slowly the Cause has grown amid all varieties of human conditions, among peoples of every religion, race and clime. In the growth and progress of the Bahá'í Cause is demonstrated its universal spiritual power. Accepted by people of every condition it is making inroads into their souls as leaven; it is uniting these many heterogeneous elements into one homogeneous world-people.

The method of Bahá'í teaching is constructive in every sense. In presenting this Cause to people, the teacher's first step, after bringing his own life into harmony with the teaching, is to confirm the seeker in the truth of his own religion and upon that confirmation, as a foundation, place the seekers faith in this latter-day teaching. Argument and dispute have

no place in this Cause. The teaching is quietly yet
fearlessly given with much love, and then the matter
is left with the listener and God. Bahá'u'lláh urges
everyone to investigate religion for himself, not ac-
cepting anything blindly nor by hearsay. People are
not urged nor enticed, but rather through the Bahá'í
spirit of love are attracted to the Cause.

All are exhorted to serve the Cause by teaching.
Contributions are not generally solicited. The spirit
of the Cause must first find root in the hearts of the
people, then they will arise themselves to support it.
When a person realizes the greatness of the privilege
of aiding the Bahá'í work, he assists in the measure
he is able, his own heart being his guide. The Bahá'ís
are working to unite all races and religions in the
love of the Lord. They are not looking for praise nor
even to see results, their satisfaction is that of service ;
and there is no other satisfaction or pleasure which
can approach that joy, - the joy of serving His Cause.

Now in these days of the first Guardian of the Cause,
Shoghi Effendi, the organization is being established
as outlined and provided for in the testament of 'Abdú'l-
Bahá. Spiritual assemblies, local and national, have
been founded and are working, as already stated, in
the many lands where the Bahá'ís are gathered. The
International Assembly, however, is yet to be inaugurated, as well as other Bahá'í institutions. Spiritual strength and confirmation in abundance attend
the early workings of the Bahá'í erganization. In
this great body of people of all races, religions, na-

tions and classes, is found the embodiment of the universal world ideal of the Bahá'í Cause; for all of these formerly heterogeneous and warring human elements are now spiritually and organically fused and united in one living cause which has for its object the living Kingdom of God here upon earth.

As there are cycles of growth, fruition and decay in life on the physical plane, there are also the cycles of birth, development, fruition, decay in religious systems or dispensations. As the cycles or seasons in the physical world are due to the condition of the material earth in its relation to the sun, so the cycles or seasons in the religious world are due to the human conditions in the world as these are affected by the divine power of the Sun of Truth or the Word of God.

Resurrection and judgment pertain to the coming of a prophet or Manifestation and the elevation of the spiritual power of religion in the world. Through the word revealed, souls are quickened and the spiritually dead are given divine life. The day of each prophet is the time of judgment for those souls who believe and adhere to the former revelations. Thus now in this day the peoples of all the religions are being tested and tried: judged, as it were. Now, as in times past, those who are clinging to the reality and truth of the revelations of the past, are finding that same truth and spirit in this new revelation, so applied as to meet the peculiar world-needs of this day and age. Those who are immersed in superstitions, are thereby veiled from the truth of this day.

In this same way was it so in the days of Christ and the prophets.

In the coming of the Báb, Bahá'u'lláh and 'Abdú'l-Bahá is found the fulfilment of the divine promises of God, given to the peoples of the past ages; and in this coming is the beginning of that age of divine enlightenment and spiritual wisdom for which men have long hoped and prayed. In the light of these inspired teachings all religious teachings of the past are understood and seen to be as parts of one great divine plan for the spiritual enlightenment of the world. In the Bahá'í Revelation is realized, also, that power which is binding and uniting the peoples of all races and religions in one universal religion which is the Kingdom of God upon earth.

Once asked regarding the relation of his mission to that of the great Manifestation, Bahá'ulláh, 'Abdú'l-Bahá replied : « Bahá'u'lláh is the root of the tree of the Kingdom, while I am the branch, branched from that pre-existent root. The fruit of the tree appears upon the branches, not upon the roots. » Now that the master, 'Abdú'l-Bahá, has passed from our midst, the Bahá'ís are realizing more the full significance of the reality of this explanation; for branching from 'Abdú'l-Bahá, the main branch or trunk of the Covenant, we find the Guardian Shoghi Effendi, the first of the line of the Bahá'í Guardians. With the passing of the generations there will be many Guardians branching out from this divine tree of revelation. The believers under each Guardian will be as the leaves, flowers and fruits of that branch (Guardian), from and through which they received nutriment and life from the tree, the root of which is Bahá'u'lláh, and the trunk of which is 'Abdú'l-Bahá. This living and ever growing and verdant tree is the symbol of the organic unity and life of the Bahá'í Cause. It admits of no division or sectarian differences or in-harmonies. Its destiny is assured. It is preordained to envelop all humanity, bringing with it the bounties of God's Kingdom to all peoples.

V.

TEACHINGS

of the Bahá'í Revelation.

Resume of the Sacred Writings with an exposition
of some of the doctrines and principles regarding
divine or spiritual education.

THE BÁHÁ'I SACRED WRITINGS
THE BÁB.

The book of the Báb, or his collective writings, is known as *The Bayán*. That the mission of the Báb was introductory to the advent of Bahá'u'lláh is most clearly stated in these writings in which the coming of « Him-whom-God-shall-manifest » is the one great theme. In them the Báb exhorts the people to prepare themselves spiritually to meet and to recognize and to adhere to Bahá'u'lláh when he should appear. He left certain laws and ordinances for the guidance of his followers until the advent of Bahá'u'lláh, which were to be abrogated with the promised « coming. » These writings, calculated to meet and minister to the local conditions which were chiefly Islamic, have as yet as a whole not been translated into English.

BAHÁ'U'LLÁH.

The writings of Bahá'u'lláh are numerous and in general are comparatively brief treatises. Of these a number have been translated and published in the occidental languages, while others still remain in the original Persian and Arabic texts.

One of the first books translated aud published in English was the Kitábu'l Iqan, *The Book of Assurance.* This was written by Bahá'u'lláh during his exile in Baghdád, and was a reply to certain theological questions asked by a learned Musl'im priest.

The expression is couched is terms peculiar to Islamic thought, yet, deeper than these terms are the universal spiritual teachings with which its pages are replete, the essence and reality of which appeals to the people of all religions.

In this book Bahá'u'lláh quotes familiar texts from the Old and New Testaments of the Bible, and from the Qur'án of Muhammad, and he explains the spiritual truths contained in these three books relative to the end and passing of the old dispensations, the coming of the latter-day revelator, and the ushering into existence of the new dispensation of the Kingdom upon earth. He points out the oneness of the teachings of the Jewish, Christian and Musl'im holy literature regarding this latter-day advent of the Promised One, the Lord.

In the Súratu'l-Haykal, « Chapter upon the Temple or Body », Bahá'u'lláh treats of the divine call, his arising in response thereto, and his mission here among men.

In the *Book of the Seven Valleys*, Bahá'u'lláh explains the different stages of the spiritual progress or development of the soul of man. These stages he divides into seven, which he terms « valleys ». This book was written to elucidate certain truths from the standpoint of mysticism. In appreciating it one understands and finds sympathy with the spirit and teachings of the Mystics.

In the *Lawh'l-Aqdas*, The Holy Tablet, « Bahá'u'lláh explains his Cause to the Christian world. He demonstrates that now is the time of the end spoken

of by Jesus, the Christ, and he exhorts the Christians
to consider the importance of this day and of its Cause.
He demonstrates the necessity for relinquishing dependence upon the superstitions in the creeds and customs
of the past ages, and exhorts all to adhere to the
pure truth of the words of Jesus, which, when understood, will confirm the truth revealed again in this
day.

The Hidden Words, in two books, — the one translated from the original Arabic text, and the other from
the Persian — contain the essence of the spiritual
truths revealed by the divine revelators of the past.

In these utterances the fundamental divine truths
are again revealed to humanity in terms applicable
to the unique exigencies of this age. These verses are
replete with spiritual significance, and in each is hidden a message, or word, for the hungry soul.

The Tablets of Tarazát, Tajall'iyát and Ishráqát,
contain exhortations regarding the conduct of man.
In these books Bahá'u'lláh dwells upon those virtues,
through the practice of which spiritually awakened
man will evolve and attain to the state of nearness
to God, which spiritual state is the foundation of peace
and prosperity.

In the *Kitábu'l Aqdas*, « Book of the Law », Bahá-
'u'lláh outlines both the material and spiritual laws
for the guidance of the people of the coming dispensation. He provides for governmental laws based on
divine laws. These divine laws are not arbitrary.
They are the spiritual principles which rule and govern
the higher or the divine nature in man, and are given

with divine wisdom. Their virtue will become apparent as men live in accordance with their statutes, and in so doing eliminate the source of the ills of the day. The ordinances of the Bahá'í Cause aim at the eradication of wrong-doing through spiritual education and evolution, and, at the same time, they protect humanity from those who perpetrate wickedness.

The Kitáb'-i-'Ahd, « Book of the Testament » is the will and testament of Bahá'u'lláh to his followers. In this document he provides for the guidance of his followers after his passing by appointing his beloved son, 'Abdú'l-Bahá, to be the Center of his Covenant, he towards whom all the faithful should turn.

Bahá'u'lláh left many other writings to the world. These are, for the greater part, in the form of epistles or tablets written to individuals. Noteworthy among these are the *Epistles to the Kings,* written just previous to his arrival at Akka, and sent from this prison to all parts of the world.

In these tablets Bahá'u'lláh declares his Cause to the kings and potentates of the earth, exhorting them to turn to the Kingdom, and to the Promised One whom God had sent to establish peace upon earth, and to inaugurate those institutions which would benefit their subjects.

ABDÚ'L-BAHÁ.

The writings of Abdú'l-Bahá are for the greater part epistles, tablets, written to individuals or to assemblies. These are explanatory of the revealed writings of Bahá'u'lláh. A number of 'Abdú'l-Bahá's lessons upon various spiritual subjects have been collected, translated and published by one of his followers under the title of *Some Answered Questions*. This work is of value to the student who desires an insight into the actual knowledge of the teachings, and an understanding of its basic principles. Several volumes of 'Abdú'l-Bahá's addresses are available in English. *Paris Talks, London Talks, The Promulgation of Universal Peace*, etc. The first two of these volumes record discourses given abroad; the latter volume, talks given in America. 'Abdú'l-Bahá's mission was that of amplifying and applying the truth as revealed by Bahá'u'lláh. This 'Abdú'l-Bahá accomplished by his life of service and example even more than by his words. His life was his book. He was endowed with that power of transmitting which enabled his followers to realize and assimilate the spiritual admonitions of Bahá'u'lláh.

In reading the translations of the writings of the Báb, Bahá'u'lláh and 'Abdú'l-Bahá, the western reader, unaccustomed to the thought and expression of the Orient, will do well to bear in mind two things: First, that these original writings were in the symbolic and florid style of the Persian or Arabic tongues; that many of the expressions and similies are untranslatable and, perforce, have been rendered literally, and that much of the rich poetic oriental expression is out of harmony with the more matter-of-fact occidental tongue, through which, in translation, it is forced to express itself.

Second, many of these epistles were sent to people surrounded by religious and intellectual conditions foreign to those to which we are accustomed here in the western world. The object of these teachers being to make spiritual connection with souls, they at one time employ a certain line of thought and terminology to reach those whom they would teach, and at other times approach their subject from an entirely different point of view. For instance, in order to reach a Musl'im the argument must be Islamic, whereas to reach a Christian it must be Christian.

In studying these writings let the reader first familiarize himself with all the conditions under which they were written : the writer, the people to whom he was writing, their previous religious training, the tongue, etc., then he will understand the spiritual wisdom of the writings, and the truth will not be obscured by the expression, names or terminology.

In order to produce world unity the Bahá'ís teach that the superstitions and prejudices of past ages must be removed from man's mind. Lack of education creates narrowness and prejudice; education brings broadness of view and sympathy with others, therefore a strong move for education is necessary.

The past systems of narrow training in matters of religion have tended more towards perpetuating than eradicating inharmony between men. The followers of the different religions being at variance with one another, have in their educational systems handed down to coming generations the prejudice, ignorance, and dogmatism of past generations, thus instilling into the children all the soul-retarding elements of thought and superstition of the parents.

Now, in this enlightened age there has appeared in the world simultaneously with the Bahá'í Revelation a new order of educational methods. Former dogma and prejudice are no longer taught to children, and the minds of the youths of this generation are not thus limited and handicapped. In fact, in freeing our educational systems from the superstitions, prejudices and dogmas of the past, the mistake of eliminating also all spiritual precepts from the general instruction of children has been made. Thinking educators of this day are beginning to see the demoralizing results of this lack of spiritual instruction in the present educational system. In the people of this generation is manifest, to an alarming degree, the inroads of vices against which they are unable to protect themselves because of the want of moral and spiritual training and poise.

'Abdú'l-Bahá taught an all-round education. Man is a combination of several natures, and his general well-being depends upon a balanced training and development. He must train and develop his physical powers in order to have a good and perfect organism through which to manifest the higher man. Psychically and mentally, he must train and develop the powers of perception, memory and reason, that he may have a mental organism through which to manifest the higher spiritual nature. Man's spiritual training and soul development is the most important of all education.

As each epoch in the spiritual progress of the world has had its divine guide or prophet who has voiced the spiritual key-note of that age, creating a religious consciousness in the heart of humanity, which is the dynamic motive force of an onward civilization, so now in this present age the world teacher, Bahá'u'lláh, has arisen, giving the universal religion, calling the whole world to one spiritual world-consciousness, exhorting all people to study into the principles and teachings of his doctrines and to enter into the spirit of his Cause.

In the light of this present day the truths contained in the teachings of the Bahá'í Revelation are self evident to those who study the writings. Humanity needs this spiritual education. Through this education mankind will become united in one world-consciousness and the universal civilization will be realized.

VI

PROPHESIES FULFILLED.

Some Biblical Prophesies showing the
Relation of the Baháʼí Revelation
To Jewdaism and Christianity

THE RELATION OF THE BAHÁ'Í REVELATION
TO JUDAISM AND CHRISTIANITY.

In the beginning of the Fourth Gospel it is written : « In the beginning was the Word, and the Word, was with God, and the Word was God. »

The Bahá'í teaches that it is through the Word of God manifested in the temple of a perfect man that humanity becomes quickened with spiritual life, obtains divine knowledge, receives spiritual assurance, is enabled to rise above the conditions of ignorance and attain both material and spiritual civilization. Thus the Spirit of God speaks and is disclosed to man through the prophets or Manifestations. Infinite Deity is beyond the comprehension of man : yet, through the Manifestation of Deity man is enabled to come into touch with God, to comprehend and to know Him through the characteristics and attributes of the perfect man or Manifestation of God, and to attain to divine knowledge which is eternal life. By this is not meant that the essence of the infinite Deity is contained or confined in the personality of the revelator, but that the soul of the Manifestation is as a clear mirror which mirrors forth or manifests the divine attributes. Everywhere in the world of nature is seen the result of God's creative power, yet this has never awakened nor brought spiritual quickening, divine joy, nor comfort to the soul of man. This is because God's creation, though it *emanates* from him, yet it does not *manifest* him. The heart of man is only divinely quickened and spiritually resuscitated through the appearance of the Manifestations of God, the Word revealed.

The Manifestation of the Word or of the Spirit through the prophets or « chosen ones, » is the unique source of the spiritual quickening and the divine enlightenment of man. This source is of God, not man. Though the prophets and divine teachers were men, their spiritual power and divine strength was not because of human virtue or wisdom. Their spiritual power to change man's nature and to create great spiritual awakening in the world was due to the Spirit of God which inspired, or spoke through, the Manifestations of God. The Word of God is a life-giving, a creative power. Through it slumbering humanity is quickened with spiritual wisdom, and the soul of man is lifted from the condition of ignorance to that of knowledge and wisdom. The advancement of the world of humanity is due to the quickening power of the Word. From it proceeds the very seed of civilization and the progress of mankind. Through it man is divinely quickened and born into the Kingdom of God.

The inner spiritual teachings of the divine Manifestations have been one and the same in substance, differing only in degree. The degree of the spiritual knowledge manifested has been always commensurate with the degree of the spiritual capacity of the peoples to whom the prophets ministered. The outer teachings, including the divine laws and ordinances of the revelators have differed in every age. These specific

instructions have always been given in conformity with
the material condition peculiar to the various ages.
The Bahá'ís regard the divine power which manifested
through all the prophets and Manifestations as the
same, being the one eternal, unchangeable Spirit of
God manifest. However, these divers Manifestations
and prophets if viewed from the human standpoint,
are seen to be different personalities, giving different
teachings and establishing different religious systems.

The laws and ordinances as given to the world by
the Manifestations and prophets have had a deep spiritual effect upon man. They were given through
divine wisdom, and by obedience to them, the living
out of the same by man, conditions were created which
were necessary for the fuller and unhampered spiritual unfoldment of humanity. It is for this reason that
each revelator has insisted that the people follow his
ordnances. It was for their own good that he commanded this. Their welfare depended upon following
his injunctions.

The prophets have been seers as well as sources of
divine life. Because of their spritual understanding
they were able to indicate in their teachings the
material signs and conditions as well as the more
spiritual ones, which would characterize the advent
of succeeding Manifestations.

The « return » of the prophets does not refer to the
return to this world of the individual person. It refers to the return in another individuality, manifesting
the same impersonal Spirit — the Word or Spirit of
God — which spoke through the prophets of the past ;

as, for example, in John the Baptist was the return of
the spirit of Elijah, but not the individual person of
the former prophet of Israel.

With the passing of centuries, people ceased to
differentiate between the individuality of the Manifestation and the Spirit of God which spoke through
him ; hence, instead of looking for the return of this
Spirit of God, manifesting through another personality,
many people in these latter days, make the mistake
of looking for the personal, individual return to earth
of their own particular prophet.

The mission of each divine revelator has been to
announce and to prepáre the way for the brotherhood
of the Kingdom among men. Each has accomplished
his mission, speaking and teaching through symbols
and parables suited to the peoples of his day. Each
quickened the souls of the people with divine life, and
each foretold the coming of the great latter-day revelator who was to establish the Kingdon of Peace on
earth.

The Bahá'ís believe that in Jesus appeared « The
Word », or the Spirit of God. This differentiated him
from other men. By virtue of the Divine Spirit which
spoke through him, he was the Christ, the Manifestation of God among men. Through him souls became
spiritually quickened, were reborn and were lifted
from the condition of spiritual ignorance, called sin,
into one of spiritual enlightenment, called salvation.

Like the mission of every divine Manifestation, that
of Jesus the Christ, was a three-fold one. First, he
fulfilled the prophecies of the prophets who preceded

him and proclaimed his coming. In him was the consummation of the former dispensations. Second, he
was the unique source of divine enlightenment to the
people of his dispensation, and through the power of
his word he founded his Cause. Third, he prepared the
way for the coming of the great latter-day revelation
fulfilled in Bahá'u'lláh — God manifesting himself
as the Father — whom he and all prophets foretold
would arise in the fulness of time and establish the
Kingdom of God upon earth.

Jesus explained the great divine plan of the ages
for the spiritualization of the world in its entirety in
the parable of « the Householder which planted a
vineyard » (Matthew 21 : 33-41), in which the householder is symbolic of God, the creator of the world.
The vineyard symbolizes the people of the world,
while the husbandmen are the leaders of the people.
His servants represent the prophets sent by the Lord
to call the world to righteousness and divine obedience,
all of whom the people persecuted and rejected. His
son is Jesus, the Christ, whose teaching was refused
by the people who crucified him. « When the Lord
therefore of the vineyard cometh, » refers to the coming
of the latter-day revelator Bahá'u'lláh while « He will
miserably destroy those wicked men and will let out
his vineyard unto other husbandmen, which shall render
him the fruits in their seasons », is prophetic of the great
outpouring of divine grace through this new revelation, which will be so great as to overcome and dispel
the great power of evil, — spiritual ignorance — which
is dominating humanity. This day is the time of the

world's turning from humanity to divinity. Bahá'u'lláh
has brought to the world a new day, for with his coming old conditions passed away and a new dispensation was ushered into existence. The law of equity,
« An eye for an eye and a tooth for a tooth », and the
Christ law of mercy and love have for centuries been
known to man, but the power to enable humanity to
triumphantly live according to the Christ law has been
given to the world through Bahá'u'lláh.

When the Spirit of God came into the world manifesting as the « Son », Jesus Christ, the world rejected
him; « but as many as received him, to them gave he
power to become the sons of God, even to them that
believe on his name ». To those individual souls he
gave his peace, but not to the world, because the world
did not receive him. This he announced when he said:
« Think not that I am come to send peace on earth;
I came not to send peace, but a sword ». Here again,
as well as in other instances, Christ states that his
dispensation was to be a militant one, which would in
the end of the age be followed by another, a triumphant dispensation of divine grace and peace here upon
earth. The history of the nineteen hundred years of
the dispensation of Christ testifies to the truth of this
prophecy of Jesus. Now Bahá'u'lláh has brought that
peace to the world. He is « The Prince of Peace »,
who has come and has established the foundation of
peace on earth. How clearly Isaiah the prophet saw
this coming of the Lord in these latter days when he
wrote: « For unto us a child is born, unto us a son is
given, and the government shall be upon his shoulder·

and his name shall be called Wonderful, Counsellor,
The Everlasting Father, The Prince of Peace ».

Those whose souls are touched by the living spirit
of Christianity, and who are alive to its reality, recognize that the Bahá'í teaching is the flowering out and
the perfecting of Cristianity; for to be a real Christian
in spirit is to be a Bahá'í, and to be a real Bahá'í is
to be a Christian. As one reads the words of Christ
and the testimony of the apostles who received from
him many teachings, there stands out one promise
above all other things: *his second coming among men,*
another appearance of the Christ spirit, the Word of
God in the temple of man as the establisher of the
Kingdom triumphant; this revelation to be the beginning of the end of the old order of human differences,
and at the same time to usher in the new order of
divine peace here on earth. All is summed up in the
promise; « the kingdoms of this world are become the
Kingdoms of our Lord, and of His Christ, and He shall
reign forever and ever ».

The Bahá'ís regard the Hebrew prophets as revealers
of divine truth. Through these various channels the
Word was revealed, souls were quickened with divine
life and obeyed the divine laws, and the way was prepared for the coming of the Kingdom on earth. These
prophets from the earliest, before Abraham, down to
the last, Malachi, formed a complete chain. Each built
upon the foundation of the teachings of his predecessors; each ministered to the spiritual needs of the people of his day, and each extended to humanity the
promise of the coming of the Lord at the end of the

days and of the righting of all things in the establishment of the reign of God among men. As one reads
the Hebrew Scriptures, the prophecies of the coming of
the triumphant Messianic dispensation are found to be
the one great thread running through all. In this promise is heard the one divine voice of the Word of God
speaking through the personalities of the many prophets or mouthpieces, or channels of truths.

In the Jewish holy books are found prophecies pertaining in particular to three holy ones to come in
these latter days. The coming of Elijah before the
appearance of the Lord, or « Ancient of Days »; the
coming of the Lord and his Servant, « the BRANCH ».

The prophecies regarding the coming of these three
holy personages were fulfilled in the coming of the Báb,
of Bahá'u'lláh and of 'Abdú'l-Bahá. Il was through the
study of the prophecies regarding the second coming, as
recorded by the prophet Daniel, that the Millerites learned that the Lord was to come in the year 1844. They
expected His miraculous appearance in the clouds and
were disappointed. The Báb came, and 'Abdú'l-Bahá
was born at this appointed time, fulfilling prophecy,
but in a manner not anticipated by men. The country of Carmel and Sharon in the Holy Land, to which
Bahá'u'lláh was sent in exile and where he lived and
taught, was the place designated by the ancient seers
of Biblical fame where the « Ancient of Days » would
appear. The glory of the Lord of Hosts to come, and
the power and majesty of his spiritual rule upon earth,
are testified to by prophet and psalmist in the most
inspiring passages of Hebrew sacred writ; while the

peace, prosperity and general upliftment of humanity resulting therefrom are most vividly depicted.

The mission of the Jewish people was a religious one. From the seed of the prophet Abraham, the progenitor of these people, have come the founders of great religions of the past, as well as the founders of the great religion of the present. From Abraham, through the line of Isaac, came Moses and Jesus; through Ishmael came Muhammad and the Báb; while from the line of another son was descended Jesse, * from whom descended Bahá'u'lláh.

* Abraham had six sons other than Isaac and Ishmael. This is not Jesse, the father of David, bnt another of the same name. This point was explained to the wirter by'Abdú'l-Bahá at Haifa, May 1910.

VII.

THE RELATION OF THE BAHÁ'Í REVELATION

To the religions of the Orient:
Islam-Buddhism-Hinduism-Zoroastrianism.

THE RELATION OF THE BAHÁ'Í REVELATION
TO THE RELIGIONS OF THE ORIENT.

As the peoples of the various religions of the Orient come into the realization and spirit of the Bahá'í Revelation, their faith in the truth of their own religion is augmented and not lessened; for the spirit of this present day teaching is the same as that which actuated the early fathers of the ancient religions, and in its doctrines, tenets, and institutions, the peoples of the former religions find the realization and fulfilment of their own holy books.

ISLAM.

The prophet Muhammad taught submission to the will of God. Islám means « submission ». Muhammad arose in Arabia at a time of spiritual need when the people were submerged in ignorance and superstition. Through his guidance, idolatry and immorality were changed into the worship of the one God and high moral standards. He brought a code of laws and ordinances adapted to the spiritual and material needs of the people of his day. These people, because of their extreme degradation, had been untouched both by Judaism and Cristianity. They needed a teaching and a code of laws suited to their own special condition. The rise of the Musl'im civilization has had no parallel in history. United under the standard of the belief in one God and the immortality of the soul, the fierce sons of the Arabian desert in an incredibly short time evolved from savagery into a highly cultured people ; their sciences, arts and literature having contributed much toward our present western civilization.

As division, superstition, and decay crept into the Musl'im Church the people retrograded, until in a few centuries after the death of Muhammad the real spirit of his teaching was a thing of the past, and Musl'im civilization was in decline.

Like Cristianity and every other religion, the real Islam must not be judged by its present day followers The student must go to the source in order to ascertain its spirit and truths. In Christianity, the building of barriers, and the divisions and wars between the sects is one thing, while the constructive teaching of Christ is quite another. So it is in Islam. The present plight of this people and the state to which the prophet called them are ideed very different.

Muhammad prepared the people for the great latterday Bahá'í Revelation. The Musl'ims look for three Manifestations in the latter day, — this being literally expressed in their traditional teachings (Hadith) as three trumpet calls. According to the traditions of Islám, seven years, and forty years, and seventy years respectively, were to separate these calls or comings.

These periods correspond to the missions of the Báb

which was cut short in the seventh year of his min-
inistry (1844-18**); to that of Bahá'u'lláh which continued forty years (1852-1892), and to that service of
'Abdú'l-Bahá which came to a close in the seventieth
year from the rise of Bahá'u'lláh in 1852 to the ascen-
sion of 'Abdú'l-Bahá in 1921.

Islam teaches of a day (a time or period) of spiritual
resurrection and judgment, and of the coming of the
Christ Kingdom, preceded by the Mihd'i, — director
or guide — and of the establishment of the divine
peace on earth. Musl'ims believe the latter-day time
of spiritual awakening or resurrection, through the
giving forth of the Word of God, to be the time of the
world's judgment, the people being their own judges,
as they choose to accept or to reject the newly revealed truth. This time was to be accompanied by certain signs similar to those mentioned in the Bible, such
as the coming of the spirit of Anti-Christ, which is
infidelity, decay of religious faith among men, and the
accompanying demoralization which this must bring
with it.

Many Musl'ims have come into the Bahá'í faith, ac-
cepting the Báb as the promised Mihd'i and Bahá'u'lláh
as the Christ (Spirit), who was to come, for both have
fulfilled their prophecies and traditions of which there
are many. According to them, the Báb appeared from
the East and made his public declaration at Mecca, at
the place and time prophesied, 18**4, A. D. or 1260 A. H.,
and taught during the anticipated length of time.
Also, Bahá'u'lláh arose in Iraq and was taken to Akka and
Carmel in Syria. His mission lasted forty years. The

many details are so clearly traced in Islámic tradition and Qur'ánic prophecy, that it is very easy for the orthodox Musl'im to realize the truth of the claims of both, and to see in their missions the fulfilment of the Islámic prophecies.

HINDUISM

The origin of Hinduism (Brahmanism), on account of the lack of annals and records in its literature, is practically lost to history. As it now is Hinduism is a most complex system of philosophical thought, manners and customs. It lacks that unity of spirit and of form which the teaching originally possessed. In all religious systems men's ideals have gradually replaced the inspired wisdom of the founders. In the religion of Hindustan this is particularly true, so that it is only with the greatest difficulty that the original spirit and teaching can be traced. Even some of the students of Hindu philosophy have doubted that originally Hinduism was a revealed teaching, for since its sacred books contain no chronicles, the personalities of the revealors have been lost. Of the truth in the original Hindu teachings, however, there is no doubt, for the voice of the spirit, the source of all religion, speaks yet today through its holy books, despite the lapse of time since they were written. The teaching in its original purity was a simple monotheism. The divine spirit spoke to the people through the mediumship of different personalities at different times. These inspired souls arose as the need for their teachings became evident among men, and they became the spiritual guides.

This thought is most clearly expressed in one of the Hindu sacred books, the *Bhagavad-Gita*, or the Lord's Song, in which it is written : « Whenever there is decay of righteousness and there is exaltation of unrighteousness, then I Myself come forth. For the destruction of evil doers, for the sake of firmly establishing righteousness, I am born from age to age. The foolish disregard Me when clad in human semblance, ignorant of My supreme nature, the great Lord of beings. » The Hindus have here one of the promises of the coming of a great incarnation, Krishna, or the Avatar, to occur in this day. He was to arise and establish universal righteousness and destroy spiritual ignorance or sin.

The latter-day Krishna was to lead the people back to the spirit of the pure teaching as given by his predecessors, (former Manifestations of the spirit of the Lord), and through spiritual wisdom and power was to overcome all unrighteousness, establishing in its place spiritual enlightenment. Those illumined Hindus whom the Bahá'í Cause is reaching, see in Bahá'u'lláh the incarnation of the Spirit of God, and they accept him as their promised one.

Thus the Bahá'í Revelation confirms the Hindu in the fundamental truth of his own religion, and frees him from the superstition and caste which have for centuries kept his people in a state of both spiritual and physical bondage. Under this influence he attains to the real spirit of sacrifice as given in his ancient teachings, and to the real emancipation of the soul, which is in truth the fundamental tenet of the most ancient Hindu teaching.

BUDDHISM.

Buddhism stands in the relation to Hinduism much as Christianity does to Judaism. Christianity sprang from Judaism - the mother religion. In like manner Buddhism came out from Hinduism. The Buddha taught of the one God, and of the life eternal. The state of nearness to God is termed *nirvana* by the Buddhists. It is synonymous with the word heaven as used in the holy writings of other religions. Gautama wrote no books. The events of his life and his words and teachings were recorded by his disciples and have been handed down to the people of succeeding generations.

Of the original teachings of the Buddha much has been lost and replaced by the doctrines and beliefs of men who came after him. In fact the latter-day Buddhist teachings, so rich in the ramifications and speculations of philosophical thought, bear about as much resemblance to the orginal spiritual teachings of the Buddha, as the present-day multiplicity of creeds of any one of the world religions bears to the real teachings and life of its founder.

The Buddhist teaching in its purity, like that of the Bahá'ís, considers all religions from the spiritual standpoint to be common truths of the one universal religion. The Buddhists are without religious prejudice. They welcome all high elevating thought and teaching irrespective of its source. They believe Gautama, the Buddha, to have been one of a series of divinely inspired souls sent to the peoples of various ages, for the divine training and guidance of mankind. As there were Buddhas who preceded him, so there will be Buddhas who will succeed him. They expect the coming and according to their traditions, he is now due. His work is to be with all mankind, and through him the earthly conditions of the past are to change and be replaced by an age of divine wisdom and understanding.

The following excerpt from the recorded teachings of Gautama to his disciple Ananda, given just previous to his death, explains in a few words much of his teaching. « I am not the first Buddha who came upon earth, nor shall I be the last. I came to teach you the truth, and I have founded upon earth the Kingdom of Truth. Gautama Siddhartha will die, but Buddha will live, for Buddha is the truth and the truth cannot die. He who believes in the truth and lives in it is my disciple, and I shall teach him. The religion which I have preached to you will flourish so long as my disciples cling to the truth and lead a life of purity. In due time another Buddha will arise, and he will reveal to you the selfsame eternal truth which I have taught you ». Ananda asked : « How shall we know him »? Gautama replied : « He will be known as Maitreya, which means 'He whose name is Kindness' ».

The Buddhists in Japan and Burma coming into the

Bahá'í Cause, find in Bahá'u'lláh the return of their promised Buddha.

ZOROASTRIANISM.

The present Zoroastrians, or Parsees, are but the remnant of a once powerful people. During the many vicissitudes of war and national decay their ancient political power has become dissipated ; through contact with peoples of other religions their original religious teaching has lost its purity, and a lifeless formalism has taken the place of its once vital spiritual force.

Zoroaster taught a pure monotheism and the future existence and immortality of the soul, all of which he explained to the people in familiar terms and parables. The physical sun, which is the source of all physical life, he used as the symbol for the Sun of Truth, the Manifestation of God, the source of all spiritual life, while the stars symbolized the lesser prophets. Purity is a fundamental teaching in Zoroastrianism. Both spiritual and physical purity are taught in its laws and ordinances, which were given in terms couched to meet the need of mankind in that ancient day. Fire being the great cleanser, it is the emblem used in this faith to denote spiritual purity, for it is through the spiritual fire of the love of God that men's souls are purified and quickened into eternal life. Zoroaster is pictured as bringing down from heaven the divine fire with which to purify mankind. The spiritual meaning

of this is apparent, although for centuries the understanding of these truths was lost, and the people igno-
rantly adhered to the outer forms, worshiping the sun,
the stars and fire, hence the term applied to them,
« Sun and Fire Worshipers ».

The same idea of resurrection or quickening. spiritual judgment and the Kingdom of God on earth,
expressed in other religious teachings, are found in
Zoroastrianism. The end of the Zoroastrian dispensation as foretold in their sacred literature, would
be characterized by spiritual impurity ; therefore the
need of another Manifestation to bring to earth the
divine fire of the love of God for the purification of
all people. The teaching has a number of prophecies
regarding the coming of the great latter-day prophet,
spoken of as Shah Bahram, and the purification of the
people of the earth by fire, — the fire of the Spirit.

The Zoroastrians in India and Persia who are now
realizing the message of the Bahá'í Revelation, accept
it as the fulfilment of the prophecies and the spirit of
their own religion, and through this teaching they
are coming into touch with kindred spirits in all the
world. Thus they are arising to perform their service
in this great work of uniting all men in the love of
the Kingdom.

VIII.

WORSHIP

— The Mashriqu'l-Adhkàr —

(The Bahà'í Temple with its accessory insitutions)
Prayer and Praise and Service to Humanity the
Elemements of True Worship.

THE BAHÁ'Í TEACHINGS
REGARDING WORSHIP.

In the Bahá'í Teachings provision is made for temples of worship, about which are to center the spiritual and philanthropic activities of the Cause, and from which will be diffused the divine teachings of the religion, together with the Bahá'í spirit manifested through service to humanity.

Eventually in every Bahá'í center there will be a building (Temple) set apart for the Lord's Cause. Grouped about this as a center will be the various institutions for the benefit of man ; hospitals, homes, hospices, colleges and other philanthropic enterprises. All of these buildings together will constitute the Mashriqu'l-Adhkár.

The Mashriqu'l-Adhkár. which translated from the Persian literally means « The dawning point of the mentionings of God, » is the Bahá'í Temple of worship and service to humanity. It consists of a central building for worship, the temple proper, surrounded by schools, hospitals and hospices, homes and asylums for the orphan, for the incurable and for the aged, and also by colleges and a university. The temple of the Mashriqu'l-Adhkár is for reading, meditation and prayer. It is essentially a place for worship, for drawing near in spirit to God. Thus it will be a center of spiritual power and attraction exerting a divine influence in the world while through the surrounding institutions will be manifest this inspiration to the world by loving service to humanity.

Its many surrounding institutions are for the practical, moral and physical service to humanity. The Bahá'ís teach that man should glorify God in deed as well as by word of mouth, therefore this principle is embodied in its fullest expression in their temples.

The central building, or temple proper, will be a nine-sided structure surmounted by a dome and surrounded by gardens. The number nine, greatest of all simple numbers, is used to symbolize the Spirit of God manifest. This universal temple of worship is open to all, here people of all races and religions can worship God individually in spirit and in truth, without the intermediary of church, priest or ritual.

The practical institutions of the Mashriqu'l-Adhkár will afford the opportunity for the establishment in the world of all branches of those progressive works for which the Bahá'í Cause stands. In this day religion is to be the direct source of inspiration in all secular affairs. The Bahá'í faith stands as the promoter of advancement in every line of human activity and development, and therefore every phase of these innumerable activities will draw life from, and be an integral part of, the Mashriqu'l-Adhkár. In the Bahá'í Teachings one finds exhortations to prayer and worship upon the one hand, and exhortations to work, and to serve humanity upon the other. « Faith without deeds is not acceptable, » therefore the Bahá'í religious work includes all work and service needful to man. This faith stands for all material and social progress, and this ideal is developed in the Mashriqu'l-Adhkár.

As one reviews history, he sees that every religion has had its temples of worship. In the epoch of the early Israelitish prophets the people led nomadic lives going up into the mountains at stated times for their religious observances; thus the open air altars on the mountains were the recognized centers of the religious life of the people.

Later, while the children of Israel were migrating from Egypt to the Holy Land, the tabernacle occupied the central position in their encampment, and subsequently, in their capital city, Jerusalem, the temple of the Lord crowned the highest hill and was the center of the intellectual, material and religious life of the people.

Still later, in the typical Christian city of long ago, the cathedral was the great central edifice about which the other buildings of the city, religious and secular, were grouped. The religious life of the people of this epoch was all important, and this principle was expressed in the architectural development of their cities, and so it has ever been in other religions.

The temple of each religion and civilization is always found to be a focal point of the city architectural. The acropolii of the Greek cities, upon the summits of which were the temples; the forums of the Roman cities with their many temples; the mosques of the Musl'-im cities; the fire altars of the Zoroastrians; the pagodas of the Buddhists; and temples of the Hindus, all testify that each religion has been creative of its own art and civilization in the evolution of an epochal temple.

As in times past true religion has been the chief motive force for advancement, learning and culture. The Bahá'ís now anticipate the day when great universal temples for the worship of God will be built, as a result of the spiritual quickening of the people, which will typify and further all progressive phases of this new age of humanity.

Some years ago the first large Mashriqu'l-Adhkar was built in the city of 'Ishquábád, in oriental Russia, where there is a considerable following of the Bahá'í Cause, and where the Russian government, both under the old regime and that of the present, has been friendly to the Cause. First, the temple proper was erected, an imposing structure in the Persian-Indian style of architecture, with its great portal facing in the direction of the Holy Land; then a school was founded, and a hospice, and now other institutional buildings are being added as the necessary ways and means are available. This work represents the combined efforts of the Bahá'ís throughout the Orient. Its architectural beauty and size testify to the loving sacrificial offerings of those believers, while the idea for which it stands is far above the conception of the surrounding people.

The Bahá'ís in America are now bulding a Mashriqu'l Adhkar. Contributions have been received from the far parts of the world sent by persons of different countries, races and religions, for the builiding of this great universal temple in which peoples of every race and of all religions might find a welcome and worship there in spirit and

in deeds. A very beautiful site has been acquired in
the town of Wilmette, just north of the city of Chicago, where the foundation and the lower story of this
edifice have already been built, and so arranged that
the building is now used for religious activities. It is
hoped that the superstructure of this temple together
with the surrounding institutions will soon be built,
so that in its completed form this Mashriqu'l-Adhkár
will stand forth as an ensign calling the attention of
the people, and attracting to its fold all those who seek
the great universal spirit of God's Cause in the world.

Of this temple, said 'Abdú'l-Bahá: « When these
institutions, colleges, hospitals, hospice and establish-
ments for the incurables, university for the study of
higher sciences and giving post-graduate courses, and
other philanthropic buildings are built, its doors will
be opened to all the nations and religions and there
will be absolutely no line of demarcation drawn. Its
charities will be dispensed irrespective of color or race.
Its gates will be flung wide open to mankind : prejudice toward none, love for all. The central building
will be devoted to the purpose of prayer and worship. Thus, for the first time, religion will become
harmonized with science, and science will be the hand-
maid of religion, both showering their material and
spiritual gifts on all humanity ».

In this service of the Mashriqu'l-Adhkar the Bahá'is
are laying a foundation for the alleviation of many
human ills the existence of which the world in general is now aware. The people of the future will understand the far-sightedness of these people of today in

their effort to bring all secular affairs under spiritual guidance. It is the foundation for the new order of the spiritual Kingdom upon earth, therefore its importance cannot be overestimated. When it stands accomplished, it will be as a haven of rest to those who seek comuniou with God within its sacred precincts; while outwardly it will be as a banner manifesting to the world the service and the purpose of the Bahá'í Cause.

Bahá'u'lláh taught that prayer and glorification of the divinity, supplemented by a pure and useful life in this world, form the elements of true worship. Faith without works is not acceptable. Every man should have an occupation which conduces to the welfare of humanity, the diligent pursuance of which is in itself an act of worship.

Not only did Bahá'u'lláh reveal spiritual laws and principles for the people of the world, but he also outlined social reforms for the more material guidance and well-being of mankind.

The ordinances of the Bahá'í faith are in harmony with the natural laws governing human relation and affairs, and are so ordered as to bring forth the highest and most perfect physical, moral and spiritual development of all who place themselves within the sphere of influence. These laws are to be followed by the people from choice, not by compulsion.

In this Cause there are teachers, but no priesthood nor clergy apart from the laity, such as one sees in some of the former religious systems. The Bahá'í teaching is given without money and without price. All are teachers, each in his own sphere of life. Those able and fitted to do so, go forth as speakers, while others teach quietly by their deeds and by speaking of the message when they find a hearer. The Cause asks only for the hearts of its followers, nevertheless, when the heart is in the work there comes the desire to give and to do something material for the movement. The giving of tithes for carrying on the work is a privilege.

Bahá'u'lláh, like all of the world's religious teachers, laid stress upon prayer and fasting. Both are necessary for the development of the soul. Through prayer the soul is brought into communion with God and receives the spiritual sustenance necessary for its life and well-being. Through fasting the soul becomes freed from the materiality of the flesh; it then apprehends higher things, becomes conscious of divine realities and receives the spiritual life forces in a higher degree than possible under the normal condition of the body.

Bahá'u'lláh clearly states that seeking refuge in creed and dogma, and faith without works, are not acceptable. The Bahá'í prayer is made individually by the suppliant to God. Prayer, supplemented by a pure and useful life in this world, forms the elements of true worship. Every one should have an occupation, which conduces to the welfare of humanity, the diligent pursuance of which is in itself an act of worship.

With the development of the spiritual world-unity, Bahá'u'lláh anticipated various universal institutions for the great benefit of humanity. He exhorted the rulers and governments of the world to abolish war-

fare and establish peace ; to settle international difficulties by arbitration rather than by bloodshed. In
order to facilitate international understanding and to
unite all people, Bahá'u'lláh advocated a universal language, which would itself be instrumental in the pro-
motion of mutual understanding and sympathy between
peoples.

From Bahá'u'lláh's writings one learns it was not
his idea that the kings of this earth should cease to
exist, but rather that all government should be established upon a system of representation, without which
no government can uphold the rights of the people.
The followers of Bahá should be law-abiding citizens
in whatever country they may dwell, and they should
be loyal supporters of all just and righteous governments.

While religion and state will never be reunited upon
the old lines of creed and dogma, the Bahá'ís look forward to the time when the states, governments of the
nations, will be based upon a spiritual foundation,
when the material laws of men will be founded and
enforced according to the principles of the divine laws
of God. Religion is necessary to man. Nations, as
well as individuals, have at times tried to live without
religion, and the results have always been disastrous.
The divine foundation is the only foundation upon
which to build any institution that shall endure. The
ideal government rests upon this foundation, which is
not a union of church and State, but a union of religion and State.

IX.

ETERNAL LIFE

The Bahá'í Teachings regarding
The Word of God,
Heaven and Hell,
The Kingdom of God.

THE BAHÁ'Í TEACHING REGARDING ETERNAL LIFE.

« The root of all knowledge is the knowledge of God : glory be to Him ! And this knowledge is impossible save through His Manifestation ». Bahá'u'lláh.

« That which is the cause of everlasting life, eternal honor, universal enlightenment, real salvation and prosperity, is first of all, the knowledge of God.» Abdúl' Bahá.

The Bahá'í Revelation teaches that eternal life is the condition of the spiritually alive or divinely quickened soul. To be merely alive to physical, animal and human things is not life according to this religious terminology. To be alive in the spiritual sense is to be quickened by, and to be conscious of, the Spirit of God manifest, to believe in him and to do according to his will.

Through the divine mission of the prophet of God, or of « the Manifestation » of God, the soul of natural man is quickened with divine or eternal life, which is as a new and higher dimension added to his human nature. By virtue of this divine quickening, and through turning to the Manifestation, the newly spiritually born soul comes directly under divine guidance. Although in the world, yet such a divinely quickened soul lives in a higher realm than before, — the divine realm — from which it receives life and a force that characterizes it with divine qualities. Thus, through the baptism of the Spirit or the Word of God revealed, the soul passes from the condition of spiritual ignorance or death, into that of spiritual awakeness or eternal life. Eternal life is not a condition to which the soul attains through its own virtue augmentative or through evolution from the natural plane. Man's capacity to receive this awakening must have its impetus through desire to know God. Eternal life is a gift and a bounty from God, bestowed upon natural man through the channel of revelation. It is given through God's mercy and favor to mankind.

There is evolution upon the natural place, but this evolution is confined to that plane. There is also evolution upon the spiritual planes, but there is no evolution from the lower plane to the higher, save through the intermediary of the life-giving Spirit which proceeds from the Manifestation. In the divine kingdom, before as well as after the physical death, there is progression towards perfection of the type of perfect spiritual manhood; for spiritual-man is the highest being of God's creation, above which there is no creation. Male and female are conditions of the physical realm and not the eternal kingdom. By virtue of the Holy Spirit, manifesting through the revealer, the souls of his followers are lifted from the lower plane to the higher plane : from natural manhood to spiritual manhood ; they become characterized with divine qualities, and they show forth in their lives the fruits of the Spirit.

As metal is heated in the fire and so partakes of the characteristics of the fire until it is like the fire, so the soul, through the revealed word, becomes charac-

terized by divine qualities. As with the heated metal, the source of the heat being outside of it,
when it is removed from the fire it loses the characteristics of the fire. So it is with the human soul;
for when the soul of man separates itself from God's
Word, divine traits cease to characterize it. The
source of human life is not man but in the Word
revealed, and the source of man's divine enlightenment
is his dependence upon the Word.

Good actions and humanitarian deeds are distinctive of
the divinely quickened soul; but good deeds are not
in themselves a proof that a soul is divinely quickened.
Many souls without faith or spiritual assurrance lead
exemplary lives according to ethical or human standards,
while, upon the other hand, many souls sunken in crime
and depravity, at the hour of death become touched
by the divine spirit, are born into the Kingdom and
bring forth the fruits of the divine life.

Life in the highest and fullest sense exists in that
soul in which all of the forces, both divine and material, reach their highest development. Neither a
physically perfect man nor a highly educated man is
upon the highest plane until he is quickened, and alive
to the divine realities. The perfect type of manhood
has an all-round physical, intellectual and divinely
spiritual development. As souls are dedicated to God's
service and become cleansed and pure from earthly conditions, then the deepest mysteries of the Kingdom
become clear to them. All doubts and fears are dispelled by faith and assurance. In this condition all
inharmonius conditions are replaced by harmonious

ones through the love of God burning in the soul. This is eternal life.

Heaven and hell, salvation and sin, light and darkness, according to the Bahá'í teaching, are terms employed to differentiate the two spiritual conditions of the soul of man. The spiritually quickened soul, alive with the life of the spirit, is that condition called heaven ; while the unawakened soul, not yet conscious of the bounty of God, nor alive in His spirit, is that state of spiritual lethargy or darkness called hell. These two conditions apply to the life of the soul in this world, as they do to the soul in the world beyond. As there are conditions of both spiritual lethargy or slumber and of spiritual awakeness here in this life, so there are these same conditions in the realm of the spirit into which the soul passes upon leaving this body.

Reward and punishment are of two kinds, natural and spiritual. In the world of nature every good act in accord with her laws, produces a good effect, and every violation of nature's principles has a harmful or detrimental effect upon the individual. The reward and punishment, the good or the bad effect following the good or bad action of man, is inevitable : it is according to fixed law. Likewise, according to the divine law, man advances spiritually, and when he violates that law he suffers spiritually. Spiritual conditions however, are more far reaching than material conditions, for they are not limited to this earthly plane ; they are eternal.

The greatest blessing which can descend upon man

is the knowledge of God. The greatest calamity is to be deprived of this knowledge. Through God's mercy He has given man the blessing of knowing Him. He has also given man free will to accept or reject this blessing as he wills, therefore divine knowledge or ignorance belongs to man as reward or punishment for his choice.

The soul is an indestructible entity which exists after its separation or freedom from the material body. Yet mere natural existence, either here or in the life beyond, is not life from the spiritual or divine viewpoint. A soul in this world may reject the light and be spiritually deprived, and at the same time be totally ignorant of its state of deprivation. From the spiritual viewpoint, a soul may be in darkness and in spiritual torment, but because of lack of spiritual perception, this soul may not realize its own condition. As darkness is but the absence of light, so ignorance is but the absence of knowledge, and spiritual death but the absence of spiritual life. Evil has no life or positive existence. It is the absence of positive light. Thus darkness, ignorance and death are negative and have no power within themselves, while light, knowledge and life are positive powers, containing those elements which dispel their opposites.

As there are many degrees of spiritual enlightenment for the soul while it inhabits the physical body, so are there many degrees for it in the realms beyond this world. In this world man is endowed with the freedom of choice. When divine grace is offered him, he can accept or reject it as he chooses. Thus his responsibility is great. Choice between light and darkness — divine illumination and ignorance — exists, however, here in this world only. In the realms beyond, these earthly conditions do not exist. There the soul can exercise no free choice, as only the good exists. There spiritual progress and development are also possible; this does not depend upon the will of the individual, but wholly upon the mercy and bounty of God. It is only in this life that man can voluntarily choose to accept the life of the spirit, and through this choice attain to divine blessings.

The Kingdom of Heaven is, both here and hereafter, for those souls who live in the Lord. Through divine revelation the promise has been extended to man at various times through the ages that in the fulness of time the quickening Spirit of the Lord, through the latter-day revelation would be so poured out upon all men of all races, that the vast majority of mankind would he illumined and quickened, and be in a state called heaven. The past conditions of spiritual ignorance and darkness would pass, and the day of divine wisdom or age of peace would come. The « end of the world, » the « destruction of the world, » and similar terms used in holy writ, are symbolic of the ages of spiritual darkness and sin, and the ushering into existence of the new epoch of general spiritual illumination. The coming age of peace, prosperity, and divine enlightenment, will be the Kingdom of God upon earth.

The Kingdom hereafther is that state of life in which the spiritually illumined souls find themselves after passing from the physical body. Man's objective senses, being of the plane of this natural realm, convey to the mind only conceptions of conditions peculiar to this material world; therefore, of that immaterial condition of the soul in the existence beyond this world man can form no mental conception whatever. As the soul attains to a greater and fuller divine life, it becomes conscious and is assured of the perpetuity and eternality of the state of awakening, and has no doubt as to the reality of the life eternal, yet cannot form a mental conception of that condition because it is beyond the scope of man's imagination.

Before the physical birth of the child into this world, it is developing its physical organs, the utility of which do not become apparent until birth. During its pre-natal life, through the mother, the child is nourished by life forces from the world into which it is to be born. So it is with the spiritual life of the soul. While in this body, the soul is developing spiritual virtues and faculties, the need for, and virtue of which, do not now appear, but will become apparent when it enters into the life beyond. Again, like the child, the soul while in this world in spiritually nourished by forces from that realm into which it will be born or enter, upon leaving this earthly condition.

The Bahá'ís believe that while so-called death in a physical sense separates souls for a time, there is in reality a spiritual link binding all souls together who are alive in the Kingdom of God and partaking of the life eternal. The souls in the realm beyond retain remembrance of things here, and interest in those dear to them. All quickened souls are spiritually united. This tie is eternal. It is not dependent upon physical means. All souls, born of the spirit, are different members of one great spiritual body, and whether those members are of this earth or in the realm beyond, there is a mystical connection between them which death does not sever. Physical ties are severed when the soul leaves the body, but spiritual ties are eternal. Through the sincere prayers of friends a soul is helped while here in this world, and likewise, through the intercession of others, a soul having passed from this life is helped on his spiritual way in the realm beyond; for progress is not confined to this earthly existence. The souls, too, who have passed on, are able through their intercession to help those here on earth. All of this is possible because the all-pervading Spirit of God is uniting the souls of the Kingdom at all times and under all conditions.

X.

WORLD PEACE.

THE BAHÁ'Í TEACHING REGARDING

Its foundation
and the means for its
realization

THE BAHÁ'Í TEACHING REGARDING WORLD PEACE

Religious differences have been one of the chief causes of warfare, while true religious sympathy and understanding have always made for peace and prosperity. Prior to the beginning of the Bahá'í Cause, little or nothing was being generally taught or written about universal peace, arbitration, a universal language, suffrage or other universal institutions. During the past three-quarters of a century, however, the universal call of this Cause has gone forth, and gradually, through much travail and suffering, the world has awakened to the necessity for all of these institutions for which the Bahá'í Cause stands. Now the accompanying lack of moral perception, is the real cause of our great world ills and of the cataclysmic conditions through which the world is now passing.

While Bahá'u'lláh's teaching was ahead of the world of his day, the world of today is realizing more and more the value of that teaching. The supply and the demand are now meeting, from which better conditions will result.

The Bahá'ís believe in a federation of all the nations, both large and small, and the establishment of a world parliament for the judicial settlement of international disputes. In treating of this matter of peace between the nations, 'Abdú'l-Bahá says:

A tribunal will be under the power of God, and under the protection of all men. Each one must obey the decisions of this tribunal, in order to arrange the difficulties of every nation.

About fifty years ago in the Book of Aqdás, Bahá'u'-lláh commanded the people to establish universal peace and summoned all the nations to the divine banquet of international arbitration so that the question of boundaries and of vital interests between nations, of national honor and property, might be decided by an arbitral court of justice.

Remember these precepts were given more than half a century ago.... Bahá'u'lláh proclaimed them to all the sovereigns of the world. They are the spirit of this age; the light of this age; they are the well-being of this age.

With the expansion of civilization and the peopling of the world, the field of conquest is so rapidly diminishing that already a new competition exists in international economic conditions. Financial and commercial relations are now becoming so intimate between nations, that cooperation must eventually take the place of the present warfare of illegitimate competition in the business world, otherwise humanity cannot continue to exist.

Owing to the present international communication and the nearness of nations, war is assuming an aspect more detrimental to all parties than it has ever had in the past. Arbitration must in the end supplant national conquest and warfare if civilization is to continue. Likewise, the warlike methods upon which the world's commerce has been and is still conducted will, ere long, become obsolete, because of the passing of the conditions which made those methods possible and profitable.

The Bahá'í Cause teaches cooperation in all affairs. Through working together for the good of the mass, rather than for the aggrandizement of the individual, the Bahá'ís anticipate that national and economic affairs will be so regulated that comparatively little misery will exist in the world. There will not be the extremes of wealth and poverty which now exist.

Through the stable financial conditions which cooperation between capital and labor will bring about — cooperation for the best good of all concerned — the laborer will be assured of a livlihood and will be enabled to get the best out of life; and, on the other hand, the capitalist will be less on the defensive and less burdened than he is now. Because of the cooperation of all classes the wealthy will occupy themselves more with matters pertaining to the general welfare of the people, rather than seeking mainly their own individual enjoyment.

As people come into the spirit of the Bahá'í teachings, see the virtue of cooperation and act upon this principle, the economic problems which now threaten the world with dire calamities will disappear and give place to institutions for the highest good of mankind, and then all people will live in harmony, in happiness, and in plenty. The Bahá'ís believe that eventually the whole world will recognize the power of the spiritual principle of cooperation, and will apply it in

matters of everday life, thus solving life's mighty
economic problem in all of its details; but this heav-
enly condition upon earth can only be brought about
by the divine power of the religion of God living in
the heart of mankind.

During many centuries the peoples of the East and
those of the West have been separated by barriers,
racial, religious, geographic and political. So complete
has been this segregation that these two halves of
humanity developed along different lines of thought,
manners and customs, until the very natures and characteristics of these peoples have become, in general,
distinct and foreign to each other.

Now, in these latter days, through the breaking
down of the former material barriers, the oriental
and occidental peoples are being forced one upon the
other. Through international relations, the increase of
foreign commerce, travel and mingling of people, the
Orientals and Occidentals are daily coming into closer
relations upon the material plane of life. As yet,
however, this is but a superficial mingling, void of
any basic unity or common consciousness. That which
will bring the Orient and Occident together is the spiritual confidence, trust, and mutual affinity and broth-
erly love which the Bahá'í faith is creating between
the East and the West. Through the establishment
of such practical institutions of service as will demonstrate this spiritual unity, the greatest material and spiritual benefit to all humanity will result; for, spring-
ing from this spiritual foundation will be all of those
religious, political, and social activities for which the

Bahá'í Cause stands, and which will eventually unite in one civilization all the peoples of the world.

The Bahá'í Cause stands for spiritual unity manifested in every sphere and activity of life. The Báb, Bahá'u'lláh, and 'Abdú'l-Bahá stood preeminent as lovers and servants of humanity. Their mission was that of spiritually uniting and giving life to humanity, therefore their teachings influence every phase and detail of life. With the fruition of their Cause which is already planted and growing in the heart of the world, the great Orient-Occident problem will be solved.

In this day the human race is reaching the stage of maturity; the Orient along its own characteristic lines, and the Occident along its own characteristic lines. Now their future development depends upon their union, both spiritual and physical. Through this Bahá'í spiritual unity encompassing all peoples, oriental and occidental characteristics will so blend that a new world-type of man will be evolved; one which will embody not only the present existing virtues of the East and West, but most of all, the higest spiritual possibilities of humanity, which can come to light only as people unite and live according to divine law applied to every phase of life.

Such a union between the East and West can never be accomplished upon any foundation other than a spiritual one. When the Occident and the Orient meet on a common spiritual ground, than an intellectual and social unity in all of its forms, with all of its institutions, will result. Many oriental countries have been held by occidental nations through physical force. This has not been conducive in any way to the solution of this world problem. Under a regime of force, both peoples, the dominant and the dominated, suffer from lack of unity. Each remains within itself, its life forces and possibilities undeveloped, pent up, and suffering for lack of the expression which only the freedom of harmony can give.

In the coming epoch of religious, racial and national unity, for which the Bahá'í Cause is paving the way, there will be no question of supremacy one over another. All peoples will be members of one harmonius world-family, each working to protect and help the others. Under this order, which is the order of God's Kingdom, the highest civic and national institutions will be evolved and the masses of the people will attain to a high state of spiritual, moral and pysical development. Thus humanity will reach a state of civilization and advancement, the greatness of which no one can now form any conception.

Going back before the dawn of history one finds the family to be the earliest social unit. Later on many families are found uniting under a patriarch, forming a clan or tribe. Still later are found federations of clans or tribes from which nations have come into existence. Now the next step is the absorbing of all national and racial consciousness into one great world consciousness. This is the order of the progress of mankind, and the great divine plan for the peace of the world; and in the fruit of the teachings of Bahá'u'lláh is seen the beginning of this great end. Civilization is the product of religion. Each of the world's civilizations had its birth in a religious movement. Civilization has always been the fruit of the spiritual awakening of a people or peoples. In this day geographic, political and social barriers have, through travel and communication, been obliterated, until now man is limited only by the confines of this planet. We are on the threshold of a universal epoch. That which affects one people politically, socially or financially, affects the whole world, and the great universal civilization so rapidly advancing is casting its signs before. In the Bahá'í teachings is the spiritual power to unite souls. It is forming a spiritual nucleus from which will spring the universal civilization to be, the magnitude of which we can now form no conception.

Today a new order of things has begun upon the earth. Mankind is attaining spiritual maturity and is demanding more spiritual food than the old forms and dogmas of religious superstitions can give him. Through spiritual enlightenment, ignorance is being dispelled, causing a change of soul, a change in man's nature, and this change is being felt the world around. The mission and object of the Bahá'í Cause is the uniting of men of all nations, religions and races in the love of God and the brotherhood of man. Its teaching is constructive. It fulfills the highest hopes of the religions of the past, and is uniting all men in the great universal religion of the future.

XI.

SOME ELEMENTS

of

The Bahá'í Philosophy

SOME ELEMENTS
OF THE BAHÁ'Í PHILOSOPHY.

The Bahá'ís teach the existence af five kingdoms ;
1. The mineral kingdom, or material plane.
2. The vegetable kingdom in which there is the
lowest apparent manifestation of spirit or life. This
plane is characterized by the principle of growth and
fruition, by virtue of which physical organisms develop
and propagate their kind.
3. The animal kingdom, the organisms of which
are differentiated from those of the vegetable plane
by the power of the five senses.
4. The human kingdom, that of man, which is
differentiated from the animal kingdom by the intellectual faculty, by virtue of which man comprehends
ideas in the abstract.
5. The divine kingdom, or condition of spiritual
illumination, which is differentiated from the human,
or natural, or spiritually veiled state of the soul,
by consciousness of God. By virtue of this higher life,
the quickened soul apprehends spiritual realities, lives
in spiritual communion with the divine, and is of the
Kingdom of God. Unlike the vegetable, animal and
human kingdoms which are dependent for development
upon earthly conditions, the spiritual life of the soul
is dependent upon the life giving force of the divine

realm. This realm is eternal; therefore the life of divinely quickened souls is eternal. The spiritual condition in which those souls live is not confined to an earthly realm.

Beyond and above all created things is the Holy Spirit of God, uncreated and infinite, unknowable to man save through His Manifestation: the mediator between God and His children here upon earth. Divinely quickened man is the highest of the creatures. From his beginning man was created man, a distinct species. In the early days of man upon earth, he resembled the animal in many respects more than he resembled the man-type of today. But from his first appearance there was in him that human spirit which, though at first hidden and not recognizable, has evolved into the type of man that we now know. In the coming age of divine evolution humanity will continue evolving to a far higher state of development than it has yet attained. Man will always be man, however. He will approach nearer and nearer to the perfect type of spiritual manhood.

According to the Bahá'í philosophy there is no scientific inharmony or conflict between these two realms of the so called natural and the spiritual, for there is perfect accord throughout the whole of creation. Natural science teaches man how to live properly upon this human plane. Through observing its laws and living in accord with them, man attains to a high state of material, physical and intellectual development. On the other hand, Christ and the prophets have revealed to humanity the laws which govern the spiritual kingdom. As people live in accord with these divine laws their souls evolve spiritually and attain to a high state of general development; for with the spiritual development follows an evolution in the natural or material development of man. When man understands the realities of both the natural and divine realms, he will find no conflict between religion and science.

As one travels in various lands, talks with the people and studies their spiritual conditions, he finds that during the past sixty or seventy years the spirit of universal or non-sectarian thought, in one form or another, has entered into the fold of practically every religion, with a tendency to break down ancient superstitions and as a leaven prepare the people for a broad universal conception of God's truth: a conception unfettered by the mental limitations of past ages. Although called by some « Modern Thought », it is in reality the most ancient of thought, for it is caused by this latter-day renewal of the spirit which the religions originally possessed, now so universally felt in all parts of the world and which during so many centuries was lost to humanity.

This general and widespread spirit of modern thought has been as a plough which has prepared the religious ground of the world to receive the spiritual seeds of universal religious ideals. Modernism has uprooted ancient creed, dogma, and much superstition; and along with this uprooting the faith of many has been shaken, and much spiritual seeking has resulted. The inspired founders of the Bahá'í Teachings have sowed seeds of a live faith in the soul of humanity. They have demonstrated to the world that faith, religion and spirituality, and that true and real spiritual principles have nothing in common with the superstitions and imaginations of the past. The modernists of all religions are teaching many of the same principles as held by the followers of the Bahá'í Cause. They realize that humanity as a whole is now passing through a period of spiritual rebirth, and that this is the beginning of a new age of spiritual wisdom. In the great spiritual organism of the universe, the various parts and members are organically united and linked together as are the organs of the body. As there have been great changes and upheavals in the evolution of the material world, due to material causes, so there have been great phases of change and development in the evolution of the spiritual world, due to the action of spiritual forces and causes.

The universal present day awakening, as seen in all of the many branches of modern thought, is the direct result of changes taking place in the spiritual realm of existence. This awakening is being mystically produced by a spiritual cause — the coming of another revelation of divine truth to man. In the early morning when the sun is yet below the horizon, the heavens are illumined by its rays and the coming of day is evident to all. As the sun slowly rises, those upon the high places see it first; later those in the valleys see it also; and when it is at its zenith, the whole country is receiving its rays and basking in its warmth.

So it is when the Sun of Truth manifests here upon
the earth for the guidance of the people. The Manifestation or revelator is preceded by the signs of spiritual awakening which show the people that a new
spiritual day or era is at hand. Those illumined souls
of high spiritual discernment first recognize in the re-
vealor or prophet the source of the light of God ; later,
the people in general awaken to his spiritual power
and wisdom ; and finally, through his teachings, both
material and spiritual bounties are forthcoming to the
world.

This wave of modernism which has swept over the
world of religion, breaking the night of spiritual ignorance and superstition, is the first dawn of the great
day of God upon earth. Already many illumined
souls are seeing in the inspired revealers of the Bahá'í
Religion the light of the world and its point of diffusion. Later on the whole world will realize that which
now only the few see. Then all humanity will be the
conscious recipients in full of the much anticipated
bounties of the Kingdom of God upon earth, for
as humanity knows and recognizes the source or the
center of divine bounty the people will turn to that
center, and through attachment to that center will
receive in the fullest measure of the divine blessings
that are being diffused in the world through the
Bahá'í Revelation.

Often Bahá'ís are asked whether or not the perfor-
ming of miracles forms a part of their teaching. In
reply they state that their belief is that the prophets
were endowed with spiritual powers which enabled them

to accomplish that which is impossible to ordinary man. The unusual things which they did were for the instruction, education and spiritual quickening of those about them. The miracles ascribed to them have been a great test of faith to the peoples of after generations, for miracles are not a proof of divinity.

The great and wonderful miracle performed by the prophets and Manifestations of the past and present, is their power to implant in the souls of man the love of God, to quicken humanity with divine life, and with all the earthly forces against them to accomplish their divine work. This is a real, a spiritual miracle.

In the writer's travels in foreign lands he found that many wonderful things are recorded by the Bahá'is, particularly those in the oriental countries, illustrative of the spiritual powers of the founders of their religion; but these form no part of the teaching, nor are they ever mentioned as proofs of divine ispiration; for if these phenomena were so presented they would prove a stumbling block rather than an attraction to truth seekers.

The spiritual insight, wisdom, and understanding of the Báb, Bahá'u'lláh, and 'Abdú'l-Bahá, which was God given and accepted by many of the peoples in their days as proof of a superhuman power, was intended for the people of these days only as the means for the quickening of their souls with a new touch of the divine life of the Kingdom. However, these incidents are now tradition, and not being recorded in the revealed word, are now legends and not a real part of this teaching.

Bahá'ís hold that a material phenomenon seemingly outside the domain of natural law would not prove to thinking people that the doer was divine. In these present days of physical and psychical experiment and research no one would ascribe divine power to the psychologist who astonished the people with demonstrations claiming to be of a miraculous nature. Were miracles a fundamental part of this religious teaching, in time to come they would become a stumbling block to truth seekers even as the same has proven true in some of the religious teachings of the past and present; therefore this phase of the supernatural is not mentioned.

The reason that science and theology have conflicted in the past, each with the other, is because many ancient theological teachings have contained so many imaginations and superstitions as to make them impossible of acceptance to science. To be sure, these superstitions did not exist in the purity of the teachings as given by Christ or the prophets themselves. Superstitions are the impediments which religion has gathered as it has been handed down through the ages. Science to day finds only this dross in contradiction to her knowledge ; but the purely spiritual teachings, though they deal with a higher realm than that of the material plane, are in perfect accord with natural science.

One finds the Bahá'í teachings to be logical and reasonable. They are free from the superstitions of the past and compatible with modern science. Those who have been privileged to travel and mingle with the Bahá'ís in many countries of the earth, find in the lives of those who follow this teaching a spiritual force which is its very life and essence. This transcends mere intellect, logic and reason, although it is in perfect accord and harmony with them. It shows scientific people that true religion not only is not opposed to science but that it is itself scientific, and that man needs more than mere intellectual food ; he needs spiritual knowledge. Not until man adds the spiritual to the intellectual has he that perfect balance by virtue of which he attains to highest development. Through the spirit of this Movement people of the old established religions realize that they have nothing to fear from the world of modern scientific thought. Under this influence the old supestitions are dropping away, and the pure, untarnished truth is standing supreme.

The realization that there is no conflict between the material and divine realm, that material truth and divine truth are in perfect accord, frees man from superstition and fear and gives him faith and assurance. This opens the door to the highest spiritual possibilities and development not only to the individual, but in the united consciousness of the mass of humanity.

The Bahá'í Cause teaches severance. In his heart man must be severed from the world and its passions. His dependence must be upon God, though outwardly he must live in the world, there fulfilling his material mission in life. In the Bahá'í life severance indicates the rebirth of the Christian, the spirit of obedience of the Jew, the submission of the Musl'im, the purification of the Zoroastrian, the sacrifice of the Hindu, the renunciation of the Buddhist, and the « living in harmony with the Divine » of the modern thinker. In the Bahá'í Cause is summed up all of the spiritual essence of the religions of the past, which is now given in a form most applicable to the present day needs of man, and adequate to cope with the modern universal problems.

The people of each religion expect the return of the spirit of revelation which shone through their prophet in the past, and they look forward to the universal establishment of their own religion. The Word of God speaking through all the prophets gave the same message of the coming of the Lord and the establishment of the Kingdom upon earth.

With each religion as time passed, and the spirit of the teachings was veiled, the people ceased to regard their prophet as a human being, the medium through whom the Spirit of God manifests. They began to deify the human personality of the prophet, and instead of expecting the return of the same Spirit manifesting itself through another personality, they began to look for the return in person of their guide or prophet. Thus the Christians believed in the corporeal descent of Jesus from the heavens, inter-stellar space, instead of the appearance of the divine power in Jesus that he promised would again manifest upon earth at the end of his dispensation. In the same way the Jews look for the personal return of Elijah « before the coming of the great and dreadful day of the Lord, » and the Musl'ims look for the personal and corporeal return of the Imam Mihd'í.

In this latter-day revelation of truth the peoples of
each of the religions are finding the fulfilment of their
prophecies and the reality of their hopes for the spiritual regeneration of the whole of divided humanity
into a great world people under a united religion of
progressive ideals conducive to the peace of the world.
The Bahá'í teachings build upon the many foundations
of the past, confirming the people in the truths of the
past, and they offer to the world the only ground
upon which peoples of all races, religions, nations
and classes can unite, the meeting ground of the
universal Kingdom of God.

XII.

THE SPIRIT OF THE BAHÁ'Í CAUSE

Its growth and development
in the Orient and in the Occident

THE SPIRIT OF THE CAUSE.

In these latter days when « prophets » and « new religions » are so abundant, one naturally wonders how to distinguish truth from error, and how to recognize the Lord's anointed One from among many men. « By their fruits ye shall know them » is the test by which the true One is recognized. The history of this Cause shows that the Bahá'í revelators overcame all worldly troubles, trials and persecutions through the power of their divine love; thus have they demonstrated their truth to the world.

They demonstrated that in order to combat evil the heart should be filled with love and truth. Fear, together with all its attending destructive forces, disappears in the presence of faith and assurance. The Bahá'í teaching is one of joy and gladness. True spirituality is profound, not depressing but uplifting. Truth and love are in the world to lift people from suffering and depression, and should therefore be presented as they are, full of joy. The Bahá'ís are taught at all times to manifest in their thoughts, words, and actions, the joy of the Lord. It is only by showing forth a joyful and happy spirit, and by a loving service to humanity, that suffering and seeking souls are attracted and brought under the power of the quickening spirit of the Cause. Through kind and loving service to all humanity, to friend and foe alike, the Bahá'ís have a most powerful weapon with which to

combat religious prejudice and spiritual ignorance.
Even the most difficult people are won through continued kindness. Once attracted, the hungry soul recognizes and accepts the truth. The Bahá'í teachers
find that when a soul is reached by their teachings,
whether a Christian, Musl'im, Jew or Buddhist, the
truth at once appeals to his inner nature, and he will
usually say, « This is exactly what I have always believed ». Thus do they prove that the language of
kindness and of the spirit of God's Kingdom is universal in its appeal. The Bahá'í faith is a world-wide
movement, the spirit of which is working unhindered
and unbound by confines and barriers of sect and
« ism ». The Bahá'ís see and recognize truth and spiritual beauty wherever found, and through this attitude of love for all they find at every hand, among
the people of other religious bodies, the opportunity
to share the spirit of their faith.

To him who has traveled and lived among the
Bahá'ís the world around, and has seen the effect of
this Cause upon the lives of peoples of every race and
religion, there can be no doubt as to the divine source
of its teachings, for in the fruits there is manifest its
truth. Among the Bahá'ís there is a practical de-
monstration of a combined religious and secular unity.
Good works are not done under the name of « charity »
or « philanthropy ». Rather it is « reciprocation » and
« interdependence ». Each gives what he has to give,
and through the spirit of giving and doing in loving
service one's own nature unfolds and he himself receives abundantly.

It has been the writer's privilege to travel and associate with the Bahá'ís in many foreign countries, and he can testify to the spiritual qualities manifested in the lives of these people. Often he has been in a position where he has been obliged to place himself entirely in the hands of strange men, whose language he could not speak, the only thing which they had in common being their faith. The connecting link was their faith, yet this was everything, because that faith was large enough to encompass all creatures.

Some western travelers whom he has met in the oriental countries were surprised that he trusted himself in out-of-the-way places and along unfrequented routes of travel, with oriental people as his sole companions and friends. When one is surrounded by friends, his personal welfare is seldom a subject of worry. The writer can truthfully state that never has he felt more at ease and free from care than when he has been with oriental Bahá'ís. Wherever he has been with them, he has always had a warmth of hospitality and kindness lavished upon him. This was not because of any other reason than that he was of their faith.

Between the Bahá'ís of the East and those of the West there exists the strongest tie. Since it was through the suffering, pain, and trials of the Bahá'ís of the Orient that this faith had its first impulse and was brought to the West, the western Bahá'ís have in their souls a strong love and gratitude for the eastern Bahá'ís and a burning desire to go to them,

and to share with them all the practical things of
the western civilization.

Upon the other hand, in the growth of the Bahá'i
Cause in the western world the oriental Bahá'ís
see the result of their labors, for the believers here
are their spiritual offspring. In us do they see the
fruit of their bloody persecution and great sufferings,
and with open and joyful hearts they are anxious to
receive into their very lives their western brothers and
sisters, learn from them and in turn pour out upon
them all of that wealth of devotion, love, and spiritual assurance which the people of the East have, and
which the people of the West need.

Particularly in the Orient the contrast between the
Bahá'ís and other people in very striking. There the
average Orientals and Occidentals meet without mingling, each remaining foreign to the other; but the
opposite is true with these very same people when
they are touched by the Bahá'i' spirit, for then we see
them associating with one another as members of one
family, having the same interests and desires, and united in the same works.

Among the oriental Bahá'ís there is a love and a
devotion to this Cause and its principles impossible
to describe. It is beyond comprehension yet one recognizes it.

In many countries and among people of different
races and religions in whose hearts the Bahá'i teachings
had penetrated the writer found such a warm welcome
and had such friendship and devotion showered upon

him, that he realized the blending process at work, which is now uniting the East and the West. This is a force working independently of material conditions and surroundings, it reaches alike the half-naked jungleman living in his hut, and the cultured man of wealth dwelling in his palace. This spiritual love, which is of God, is the strongest power in creation. In its uniting force is the foundation of accord and harmony upon which the Orient and the Occident are meeting. From this Cause will appear, as fruits, all of those social institutions between the East and the West which will materially demonstrate the truths which the Bahá'ís now witness as spiritual realities.

The Bahá'í teaching encourages marriage, while asceticism and celibacy are discouraged. Monogamy is taught, and among the believers in the Orient is gradually replacing the systems of polygamy, which, from time immemorial, have existed in those countries. The human body should be developed, not mortified, because it is the medium through which the spirit works. A good and perfect body is desirable as a means for serving God.

Bahá'u'lláh strongly denounced the taking of opium and kindred drugs. The Bahá'ís do not use intoxicating liquors as beverages, and among them even the use of tobacco is discouraged. Gambling is forbidden as having a demoralizing effect upon the people. In fact, all excesses tending to weaken the body and the moral force of man should be eschewed by him.

Individual advancement and personal incentive are to be fostered and encouraged, but the general weal

of the mass is even more to be considered. The weak
and unfortunate ones are to be protected from the
greedy ones. Profit in business is to be sought, but one
person has no right to enrich himself at the expense
of others. When the ordinances of Bahá'u'lláh are
established, there will be fewer extremes of wealth and
poverty. All the people will be more tranquil and
secure than they are at present. The Bahá'í Cause is
prepared to meet and to reform the many human
ills that the humanitarians and workers of the day
are striving to eradicate. This is being accomplished
through the spiritualizing method of changing the natural hardness of man's heart by infusing into it the
love of God.

As people know and understand the wisdom of
the precepts of Bahá'u'lláh, they will from volition and
for their own welfare and that of those about them
desire to live according to his advice. Perfect liberty
and freedom in religious thought and belief is allowed
everyone. The Bahá'ís are exhorted to mingle freely
with people of all creeds, and in no way to shut
themselves off from those of other beliefs. Neither
should they criticise nor denounce the teachings nor
the followers of other religious movements. Through
fraternal intercourse, kindness and loving service to all
humanity, the believers in this latter-day revelation
will eventually demonstrate its truth to all the world.

Often people inquire whether affiliation with the
Bahá'í Cause necessitates the giving up of church
membership. The advice is always that no human or
religious relation should be severed, but that these

relations should become as avenues for the giving forth of the new message, and the spirit of the Bahá'ís having church relations should coutinue to mingle with church people. However, they do not remain silent about the new light which has come to them. When they meet people who are seeking and hungry for the teachings they give to each to the limit of his or her capacity. Where people are satisfied with their own religious opinions, they give them what they can without arousing their antagonism, allowing the seeds of the message to enter as leaven into their thought, with the assurance that in time spiritual fruits will be forthcoming.

While the Bahá'ís are taught not to interfere with the religion of others, all people are exhorted and advised to relinquish those creeds and customs which separate them into many divisions, in order that all may come into the one great spiritual unity of the Kingdom. All things find their strength in unity. The life of any being or organization of beings is dependent upon this principle. Therefore, how important is unity ; and of the various degrees or kinds of unity how all-important is spiritual and religious unity, for it is the foundation of all real unity and of the progress of the world.

In carrying on the Bahá'í work the world around, it has been found when two or more come together to discuss religious matters with perfect love in their hearts, the result is always uplifting and edifying. When people meet together for religious discussion without this spirit of true charity in their hearts, the result is always disturbing and distressing, and it would have been better had they not met. This principle of the power of love the Bahá'ís know and they rely upon it and not upon arguments presented from the plane of intellect alone.

The most potent of all factors in moving humanity is love ; it is at the same time the most elusive and the most difficult of all things to define. We know it only through its characteristics, and these we never fail to recognize. So it is with true religion. Therein is a spiritual force working which is divine love. This is its very life force. When one feels his soul responding to this, he realizes that he has come into contact with a higher realm, and though he cannot describe this awakening in so many words, it is none the less the most real of all things.

In the Bahá'í Cause woman hold a position equal to that of man. She is not denied any rights. Through the Bahá'í teachings woman in the oriental countries is even now reaping the benefits of education, and advancing in many ways which the customs of former religions closed to her. It is hardly necessary here to mention those Bahá'í laws and ordinances which touch upon hygiene and education of both sexes, and the admonitions forbidding mendicity, slavery, cruelty to animals and other offenses, because our western civilization has already accomplished these reforms though in the Orient the need for them is yet very great.

The Bahá'í teaching stands for the higher education of woman. In some instructions sent to the Orient, 'Abdú'l-Bahá exhorted the Bahá'ís to give their daughters every possible educational advantage, telling them it was even more necessary that their girls should be educated than their boys, because women are the mothers and the natural teachers of men, and it is of the greatest importance to the race that they be highly educated. Already several American Bahá'í women physicians are working in Persia. Their influence is of the greatest importance among the women, because they are able to penetrate into the seclusion of the family life of the people in ways not open to men.

Other American Bahá'ís have gone to Persia as teachers, and are associated there with the educational work of the Cause. Some time ago a girl's school was opened by the Bahá'ís in Tihrán, and from the last accounts there were more applicants than could be accommodated. Educational work is being carried on in all of the oriental countries where there are congregations of believers. Each year also brings Bahá'í students to Europe and America, who after completing their studies return to their own countries as teachers. Through liberal education and the diffusion of knowledge and wisdom, both spiritual and material, the superstitions and limitations of the past will cease to exist, all people will be in sympathy with humanity as a whole, and each individual will consider himself a citizen of the world rather than confine all of his interests and sympathies exclusively to one country and one people.

In Persia the writer found the Bahá'ís struggling against great opposition, upon the part of those surrounding them, in their work of uplifting and educating woman, and he met Bahá'í women who are doing great work for their own sex. Until comparatively recent this work, for the most part, has been very quietly done, — in fact, almost in secret, — on account of the persecutions by the Musl'ims. The Bahá'ís are undermining those traditions regarding the seclusion and oppression of women and now the Bahá'í women in the Orient are progressing rapidly.

The Persian Bahá'ís are a most staunch and courageous people. While the massacres and martyrdoms of great numbers of Bahá'ís in that land are probably now a thing of the past, nevertheless, they are still under persecution which even in these days often leads to loss of life. Many men whom the writer met had been eye witnesses of the massacres of the 60's in which so many of these people died for their faith, while others with whom he talked had lost family, friends and property. One impression which the writer recalls very vividly, was the calm way, free from any trace of rancor, in which the Persian Bahá'ís referred to the losses and afflictions visited upon them by the enemies of the Cause. Instead of causing embitterment, these troubles have had a most spiritualizing effect upon the believers: the persecution has been as a fire which has taken everything from them save the love of God, with which their hearts are ablaze.

After a visit among these people, one feels spiritually better and stronger than before, absorbing a force from them which gives spiritual courage in moments of weakness, and guidance in moments of strength. This is the spirit which abides with those who are in reality severed from all save God. It is this spirit which is manifest in the life and teaching of the revelators of this Cause, and in the lives of those who in spirit follow the principles for which they stand.

CONCLUSION
□□□□

TESTIMONIAL OF A TRAVELER.

Visits made to 'Abdú'l-Bahá. Development of the principles of the Bahá'í Cause, the method of teaching, and its growth in the Orient.

TESTIMONIAL.

In the preceding articles of this series I have attempted to give a general resume of the history and teaching of the Bahá'í Cause, and the work now being accomplished by its teachers in various parts of the world. In conclusion I desire to relate a few of my own experiences in connection with this Cause. During the past twenty-five years it was my privilege to be in intimate contact with the workings of the Movement, having been permitted to visit 'Abdú'l-Bahá several times, and to travel extensively among the Bahá'ís in foreign lands. It is with the desire of sharing the inspiration received from 'Abdú'l-Bahá and from his followers that I am presuming to record these personal observations.

My first visit to 'Abdú'l-Bahá was in the winter of 1901. At that time the Cause in the West was in its infancy. But few of the words of Bahá'u'lláh and 'Abdú'l-Bahá had been translated, and the then few believers, though fired with faith and a great desire to disseminate the teachings, had as yet learned but little of the teachings and spiritual principles of the Cause, with which philosophy many are now familiar.

At that time 'Abdú'l-Bahá was in comparative freedom. Having been allowed to leave the prison city of Akka with its unhealthy climate, he was spending the winter in the neighboring town of Haifa. Notwithstanding this betterment in the conditions of his daily life, one felt the weight which was upon his soul, and one saw how taxed he was in his many endeavors and continued efforts in teaching and training the people in the path of Bahá'u'lláh. Receiving people by day and carrying on a large correspondence which necessitated his laboring far into the night, one marveled at his powers of physical and mental endurance; but as one obtained glimpses of and received the spiritual fragrance from the great soul of 'Abdú'l-Bahá, one had moments of realization that his strength was not from the human man, but flowed through him as through a channel, coming from the invisible power of Bahá'u'lláh which he always testified was the source of his inspiration.

For over a year before I first met 'Abdú'l-Bahá, I had been a believer in the Bahá'í Cause, so when I went to him it was not to have my faith established, but rather to have a spiritual confirmation and to gain more knowledge. From the moment I met him I realized that he knew my innermost soul, thus a spiritual bond was established which has never ceased to be a source of joy, delight and help to me. Successive visits with him, and each tablet (letter) and message received from him, strengthened this understanding and demonstrated to me again and again 'Abdú'l-Bahá's all penetrating spiritual insight and wisdom. Notwithstanding the distance and circumstances which separated 'Abdú'l-Bahá from his friends, when they received his tablets they found advices and admonitions peculiarly applicable to them in their needs of that moment; and even now that he has departed from this world one finds this spiritual nearness or connection to be ever very real and powerful: one attaining to it in proportion as he arises to serve in the path of 'Abdú'l-Bahá, according to the teachings and behests.

During the eleven days I remained in Haifa on my first visit, I had 'Abdú'l-Bahá's personality and spirit deeply engraved on my consciousness. All was not easy to understand; I had many questions; but shortly before I left him everything seemed to become very clear, — my spiritual rapport with him was established. The moment of our parting was a most happy one, rather than distressing for me. I felt that I was carrying away with me something which would never be destroyed, a spiritual friendship which would grow eternally both here and in the realms beyond.

Early in the summer of 1901, shortly after my first visit, conditions arose which necessitated the return of 'Abdú'l-Bahá to the prison city of Akka. There he remained for seven years, with the exception of short periods upon several occasions when he visited the tomb of Bahá'u'lláh at Bahjí, a mile or two beyond the city gates. During this period of imprisonment it was at times with the utmost difficulty that pilgrims were able to see him; nevertheless this was a time of great growth in the Cause. 'Abdú'l-Bahá worked very diligently with his pen directing the onward march of the Cause in distant lands, and the result of his labors became apparent among the Bahá'ís in all parts of the world: they were receiving from him that quickening spirit of religious enthusiasm and faith which is now so clearly manifest in the growth of his Cause in many parts of the Orient and the Occident.

Six years elapsed between my first and second visits to the Master, 'Abdú'l-Bahá, during which interim he had been confined to the fortress. Knowing that some recent pilgrims had remained nine days in Akka, I had rather set my heart upon a visit of the same length. Reaching Haifa I was told that on account of the troublous conditions surrounding 'Abdú'l-Bahá I would be able to remain with him but a few hours, and that even this short visit could be arranged for with much difficulty. At first the thought of so short a visit was a keen distress and disappointment. Upon second thought, however, I realized that 'Abdú'l-Bahá was above material conditions, although seemingly held by them; that in reality he was free and master of the situation and was planning for the best; and that even under these conditions I would be able to get all that my soul needed at that time.

Whether or not one benefitted by meeting 'Abdú'l-Bahá depended upon the real or soul contact. It was the open, unprejudiced and seeking souls who united with the soul of 'Abdú'l-Bahá. When this spiritual contact was effected, through turning to him in spirit and serving in his Cause, the personal visit to him was not essential for enlightenment; for with spiritual connection between the soul of Abdú'l-Bahá, who was the heart of the Bahá'í Cause, and the believers, the members of the body of the Cause were one with him. Through this unity his divine wisdom and love went forth to all his followers.

Although this my second visit with 'Abdú'l-Bahá was very short, I would not have wished it otherwise. Again I left him in great joy, with my soul overflowing with the love of the Kingdom which he so freely radiated. The one great lesson which he taught me at that time, as I recall it, was dispelling negative fear with positive assurance. The natural tendency of many people is to close the door of the heart to others, and to shut themselves away from people. This becomes a habit, and one which causes much distress and suffering, because humanity is one whole and its health and proper functioning depends upon a free and frank interchange of thought and good feeling, free from repression and constraint. Rather through his manner and the way in which he received and treated me than from anything which 'Abdú'l-Bahá said to me, I saw clearly that the way to serve him in the Cause was never to remain aloof from people, but literally to attack humanity with a good spirit of love and grace. I saw that it was because of 'Abdú'l-Bahá's freedom from constraint, and his fearlessness and friendly way of approaching people, his frank expression of love, faith and assurance, that he was able to reach the souls of men and impart to them his courage and wisdom and to break down the barriers of separation.

'Abdú'l-Bahá entered into the lives of all about him. Through this contact he undoubtedly suffered

much, nevertheless he was enabled thus to reach the
people and to minister to them. His life was a lesson to
all, for in his method one saw the way in which the
Bahá'ís must live in order to do their work among
men.

My next visit to 'Abdú'l-Bahá was during the climax
of his troubles and difficulties, just previous to the fall
of the old despotic Ottoman power and the re-establish-
ment of the constitutional government in the midsummer
of 1908. Upon arriving in Haifa I found that some
recent American pilgrims had not been able to meet
'Abdú'l-Bahá, but had returned to America happy in
having seen him from a distance as he walked upon
an elevated balcony on his house within the fortifications of Akka. Four Arabs, recent converts to the
faith, had for several months been confined in the
prison fortress on account of their belief. Others of the
Bahá'ís, in order to avoid pending trouble, had by the
Master's advice sought temporary refuge in Egypt;
while those remaining in Syria were all but panic
stricken by the trouble and persecutions which were
daily descending upon the Bahá'í community from the
hands of the unscrupulous government officials.

After I had waited several days in Haifa, word
came from 'Abdú'l-Bahá for me to go to Akka and
proceed to the house of a certain Persian, one of the
oldest and most faithful of the believers. In the guise
of a native Syrian, wearing fez and aba, with the
assistance of one of the oriental Bahá'ís, I entered the
prison city, passing through the guarded gates along
with a small crowd of comers and goers without being

halted. Once established in the privacy of the house of the Persian friend, 'Abdú'l-Bahá, having the freedom of the city within the fortifications, came to see me several times. Although under the most severe physical difficulties, he was visibly in the greatest spiritual strength and power. In strong contrast with the fear and terror of his followers for his safety, impossible to describe, 'Abdú'l-Bahá stood forth in the greatest joy of soul and tranquility of spirit. He radiated calmness and assurance and through his strength the community of the friends was saved from despair. The situation was dramatic in the extreme. It was shortly followed by the tragic downfall of the government that for forty years had held 'Abdú'l-Bahá a prisoner.

Several months later I was again permitted to travel in Syria and visit Abdú'l-Bahá. Although it had not been long in point of time since my previous visit, yet the conditions surrounding 'Abdú'l-Bahá had so changed as to make the previous time seem, by comparison, to have been in some former decade. 'Abdú'l-Bahá was free! The uttermost liberty existed. Akka had ceased to be a penal colony and the gates were no longer guarded, but wide open to the world.

The Bahá'ís had not yet recovered from their first ecstasy of joy over the freedom of 'Abdú'l-Bahá, yet through all this manifest jubilation he was conducting his work as usual. It was then that I realized, to the extent of my capacity, how far above this world's conditions 'Abdú'l-Bahá stood. Not discouraged by criticism, persecution, calamity; not elated by applause, commendation or good fortune, he was apart from the ever changing world of human affairs, upon a firm rock : the spiritual foundation of the Kingdom. By virtue of this severance from all save God he was enabled to change the interest of the people from the world's thought, and from materiality to spirituality, and to create in men's souls the fire of God's love.

Almost two years after the great change of government in Turkey I again went to Syria. In coming in contact with 'Abdú'l-Bahá, each soul receives the message or the lesson for which it is then at that time ready and prepared to receive. Previously my attention had been chiefly called to those principles for which 'Abdú'l-Bahá stood, which are so clearly manifested in his life, while my mind had not dwelt much upon his personality as a man. Now this, which previously I had allowed to pass almost unnoticed, was to be my chief lesson. My attention focused upon the exquisite beauty of 'Abdú'l-Bahá's personality, — from lines of physical strength and refinement in his face to his trained thought and judgment. His dignity and carriage, his mental grasp of things both great and small, and the manner in which he dealt with them in proportion to their importance, were all of the deepest interest to me. In his person one saw at once the power of the spirit of Bahá'u'lláh has well as its gentle refining qualities, — a combination of strength and delicacy of masculine and feminine qualities; the balanced combination of dignity, humility, forcefulness and gentleness.

Whatever was one's mental conception of 'Abdú'l-Bahá, one invariably had to readjust it from time to time.

Under his guidance his followers were growing in spiritual stature, and as the perceptive powers of their souls increased, they saw more and more clearly 'Abdú'l-Bahá's spiritual power and divine mission. Did one visit him many times, each time his former idea of him would be laid aside for a clearer and a more definate conception.

Again I visited 'Abdú'l-Bahá in September, 1921, during his sojourn in London. There he was in the vortex of western civilization, sought by many people from various walks of life both high and low. Under these conditions his spirit shone forth with greater brilliancy than ever before. It is natural and easy for the western mind to weave a halo of sentiment and romance about the personality of a persecuted religious leader, exiled and imprisoned for his faith under the corrupt rule of an oriental despot; but when this same spiritual teacher comes into the limelight of western thought and customs, the people see him from a different angle; things which they but imagined about him are dispelled and his real virtues stand out more strikingly visible than ever.

'Abdú'l-Bahá in London, out of his accustomed oriental environment, appeared more clearly than ever the master of the spiritual situation. I heard him give the first public address that he ever made. This was before a vast concourse of about 2,000 souls, gathered in the City Temple in London. I was also with him during a number of personal interviews granted to various truth seekers. At all times under these unaccustomed conditions he drew unto himself people of all kinds and types, from the humble and unschooled, to the intelligencia; and through his love, wisdom and power, gave them spiritual assurance and satisfaction.

Many friends of the Cause in America cherish vivid remembrances of the visit of the Master to the United States and Canada in 1912. His travels there lasted for eight months, taking him from coast to coast, and was the most memorable incident in the lives of the Bahá'ís on that continent, the effect of which cannot be expressed in words, the realization coming only as one is conscious of the work and the service to the Cause which 'Abdú'l-Bahá accomplished during that period. Many able pens have recorded the details of these travels; but more indelible than these annals is the ever living spiritually quickened enthusiasm of faith in the Cause of Bahá'u'lláh, which the Master planted and left growing in the hearts of the believers in the western world.

Almost two years after 'Abdú'l-Bahá left America, I was privileged to visit him again in the Holy Land, to find him calm and unagitated in the midst of troublous and tumultuous human conditions. It was in the fall of 1914. The war was on. Turkey was getting ready to enter the combat, and Syria, then a Turkish domain, was all confusion and disorder, torn by opposing and conflicting war propaganda, with the people in a deplorable state of fear, anxiety and terror. Amidst all this confusion the Master 'Abdú'l-Bahá stood for calmness, assurance, and the protection of the people.

I left Haifa shortly before Turkey went into the war, and it was not until January 1921, over six years later, that I saw 'Abdú'l-Bahá again, and for the last time. The strain of the terrible years of the war with its psychological tension and physical privations had left its traces written upon his benign countenance. But now all was different in the Holy Land and a new epoch of tranquility for the Bahá'ís had arrived. The English Government in acknowledgment of the services of 'Abdú'l-Bahá to the people, and his influence in maintaining harmonious relations between adherents of the many clashing and opposing religious interests in Palestine, had tendered him the order of Knighthood of the British Empire, and this he had graciously accepted. From that time he became officially known as Sir Abbás Il-Bahá'í.

This was the evening of the Master's thirty-year mission, but he was in no way resting from labor. His great work had been done; people now were flocking to him from all parts of the world, each day bringing pilgrims singly and in groups. Under these conditions he was busier than I had seen him on any of my previous visits. It was superhuman strength that permitted him to stand the strain of the many interviews and visits, the multitudinous details of the now expanding Cause which necessitated his working late into the night and arising early in the morning in order to carry on his corrispondence alone. Through the human veils of this busy existence one saw towering within him the spiritual forces of El Abhá, and at times one seemed to get a fleeting glimpse into the depths of his wisdom. Ephemeral and evanescent as was this impression one felt the profoundness of the power of the Spirit within him and one was awed in Its presence.

The Master had gone to Tiberias in Galilee where he had work to do, and from there he called me and my brother from Haifa for a two-days visit with him before sending us back to America. Our route took us to a point on the southern end of the lake where we embarked in a boat which took us to the town of Tiberias, about midway up the lake on its western side. Off to the north we could see Capernaum, above which in the distance arose the snow covered top of Mount Hermon; while between Capernaum and Tiberias we could distinguish the crumbling ruins of Magdala. The Sea of Gennezareth, which at times is very rough, was smooth enough to reflect the mountains which rise abruptly in places from the shores. The entire scene was one of tranquility and peace, conducive to meditation and thought which took us back over the nineteen hundred years when the Master, Jesus, and his disciples walked and taught upon those shores. And we were approaching that same ground upon which now stood 'Abdú'l-Bahá, upon whose shoulders was the mantle of the Lord, the one who in this day voiced the message of the Kingdom, calling all men of all nations to the table of the Lord; the one who had drawn into one faith peoples of all religions, laying a foundation in the heart of humanity and building a Cause which is destined to grow until it encompasses the world, fulfilling the promises of the Christ and the prophets of the past in ushering in the millenial age of happiness and peace upon earth!

Forty-eight hours replete with divine significances, immersed in the atmosphere of his love, and then we were receiving 'Abdú'l-Bahá's parting embrace, instructions and blessing, and turning our faces from him on our westward way to our field of work in America. As always upon leaving the Master my heart was happy. We had attained to his meeting and our hearts were satisfied. Our cups had been filled to overflowing with his spirit and his love and we were starting forth on our mission to share this divine bounty with those who were hungering and thirsting for the faith and assurance which had been so bounteously vouchsafed to us. Our blessing was complete. For what more could we have wished?

My last visit to the Holy Land was a year after parting with the Master. In the meanwhile he had ascended to the Supreme Concourse, and the hearts of his friends were heavy and weighed down with the grief of this separation. I approached Haifa sick at heart, feeling too depressed for words, knowing in my consciousness of soul that 'Abdú'l-Bahá's Cause would live and prosper in the world, but without understanding or knowing how this was to be accomplished.

A few hours after my arrival the beloved Guardian of the Cause, Shoghi Effendi, gave me a copy of the Master's Will and Testament to read and to study. This was the first access I had had to this most holy document. Like all of the Bahá'ís I found therein spiritual confirmation in the great divine plan, — the way outlined by the Master for the continued guidance and furtherance of his Cause. Furthermore, in the institutions of that plan under the guidance of the appointed Guardian, Shoghi Effendi, I found the channel through which 'Abdú'l-Bahá's life-giving spirit is now functioning and continuing to give divine life and guidance to his Cause here on this earth, and this brought assurance and tranquility to me as it has to multitudes the world around.

We are now in the early days of the New Age of the Kingdom upon earth, and the guidance of God is for all those who realize this and work and serve in harmony with the great divine plan of the past ages which finds its consummation in the Bahá'i organization founded by 'Abdú'l-Bahá, now the center of guidance for unity, harmony and understanding between the peoples of all nations, races, and religions.

FINIS.

Catalog of Bahá'í Literature

Writings of Bahá'u'lláh

Hidden Words, the essence of the teachings of all the Prophets.
Paper covers . . . . $ .25
In leather. 1.00

The Book of Assurance, (Tablet of Íghán), explaining the oneness of all the Prophets and their significance as the expression of the Will of God . . . . . . $ 1.50

Tablets of Bahá'u'lláh, (Tarazát, The World, Words of Paradise, Tajall'iyát, Glad Tidings, Ishrágát), social and spiritual principles of the new age . . . . . $ 1.75

Seven Valleys, the stages passed by travelers on the path of spiritual knowledge . . . . $ .25

Writings of 'Abdú'l-Bahá

Promulgation of Universal Peace, public addresses delivered throughout the United States in 1912, Volume One . . $ 2.50

The Wisdom of 'Abdú'l-Bahá, a brief but complete presentation of his message. Paper covers . . . . . . $ .40
In cloth 1.00

Some Answered Questions, an exposition of fundamental spiritual and philosophic problems . . . . . $ 2.00

Tablets of 'Abdú'l-Bahá, intimate letters written in reply to questions addressed by individuals and groups. . . $ 1.75

Mysterious Forces of Civilization, a work addressed to the people of Persia nearly forty years ago to show them the way to true progress . . . . $ 1.15

Divine Philosophy, selected addresses delivered in Paris on the eve of the Great War . . . . $ .75

'Abdú'l-Bahá in London, a record of public and private addresses delivered in 1911 . . . . $ .75

'Abdú'l-Bahá in New York, containing selected addresses delivered at Columbia University and various churches and public meetings in 1912 . . . . $ .25

Tablet to the Committee on Peace, The Hague, a letter written in 1917 to reveal the foundations of universal peace . . . . $ .10

Wisdom Talks of 'Abdú'l-Bahá, selected addresses on spiritual and scientific subjects. . . . . $ .10

Compilations

Bahá'í Scriptures, ... $ 5.00

Books about the Bahá'í Movement

The Bahá'í Proofs, by Mirza Abul Fazl Gulpaygan . . $ 1.50
The Brilliant Proof, by Mirza Abul Fazl Gulpaygan . . $ .25
Bahá'u'lláh and the New Era, by J. E. Esslemont . . . $ 1.50
Bahá'u'lláh and His Message, by J. E. Esslemont . . . $ .20
The Oriental Rose, by Mary Hanford Ford, ... $ .80
Unity Triumphant, by Elizabeth Herrick, ... $ 1.50
Bahá'ísm: The Modern Social Religion, by Horace Holley, . $ 2.50
Bahá'í: The Spirit of the Age, by Horace Holley . . . $ 2.50
The Revelation of Bahá'u'lláh, by Isabella D. Brittingham . $ .15
A Series of twelve articles introductory to the study of The Bahá'í Teachings, by Charles Mason Remey.

184 pages - bound in Cloth . . . . $ 0.50
10 copies . . . . $ 4.00

The Universal Consciousness of The Bahá'í Revelation, by Charles Mason Remey.

60 pages - paper board covers . . . . . . $ 0.20
50 copies . . . . $ 9.00
100 copies $16.00

These book can be purchased from the

BAHÁ'Í PUBLISHING COMMITTEE

P. O. Box 348   **Grand Central Station**

New York, N. Y., U. S. A.